THE BOX-CAR CHILDREN

Gertrude Chandler Warner

Copyright © 2021 Public Press

No rights reserved

The characters and events portrayed in this book are fictitious. Any similarity to real persons, living or dead, is coincidental and not intended by the author.

This work is in the public domain. No copyright claim is made with respect to public domain works.

ISBN: 979-8-7791-2999-2

CONTENTS

Title Page
Copyright
THE FLIGHT   1
THE SECOND NIGHT   7
SHELTER   13
A NEW HOME   18
HOUSEKEEPING   24
EARNING A LIVING   30
AT HOME   37
BUILDING THE DAM   43
CHERRY PICKING   49
THE RACE   54
MORE EDUCATION   60
GINSENG   66
TROUBLE   70
CAUGHT   77
A NEW GRANDFATHER   82
A UNITED FAMILY   87
SAFE   92
About The Book   95

About the Author

THE BOX-CAR CHILDREN

By

Gertrude Chandler Warner

Jess shut the door with as much care as she had opened it

THE FLIGHT

About seven o'clock one hot summer evening a strange family moved into the little village of Middlesex. Nobody knew where they came from, or who they were. But the neighbors soon made up their minds what they thought of the strangers, for the father was very drunk. He could hardly walk up the rickety front steps of the old tumble-down house, and his thirteen-year-old son had to help him. Toward eight o'clock a pretty, capable-looking girl of twelve came out of the house and bought a loaf of bread at the baker's. And that was all the villagers learned about the newcomers that night.

"There are four children," said the bakeshop woman to her husband the next day, "and their mother is dead. They must have some money, for the girl paid for the bread with a dollar bill."

"Make them pay for everything they get," growled the baker, who was a hard man. "The father is nearly dead from drinking now, and soon they will be only beggars."

This happened sooner than he thought. The next day the oldest boy and girl came to ask the bakeshop woman to come over. Their father was dead.

She went over willingly enough, for someone had to go. But it was clear that she did not expect to be bothered with four strange children, with the bakery on her hands and two children of her own.

"Haven't you any other folks?" she asked the children.

"We have a grandfather in Greenfield," spoke up the youngest child before his sister could clap her hand over his mouth.

"Hush, Benny," she said anxiously.

This made the bakeshop woman suspicious. "What's the matter with your grandfather?" she asked.

"He doesn't like us," replied the oldest boy reluctantly. "He didn't want my father to marry my mother, and if he found us he would treat us cruelly."

"Have you ever seen him?"

"Jess has. Once she saw him."

"Well, did he treat you cruelly?" asked the woman, turning upon Jess.

"Oh, he didn't see me," replied Jess. "He was just passing through our—where we used to live—and my father pointed him out to me."

"Where did you use to live?" went on to the questioner. But none of the children could be made to tell.

"We will get along all right alone, won't we, Henry?" declared Jess.

"Indeed we will!" said Henry.

"I will stay in the house with you tonight," said the woman at last, "and tomorrow we will see what can be done."

The four children went to bed in the kitchen, and gave the visitor the only other bed in the house. They knew that she did not at once go to bed, but sat by the window in the dark. Suddenly they heard her talking to her husband through the open window.

"They must go to their grandfather, that's certain," Jess heard her say.

"Of course," agreed her husband. "Tomorrow we will make them tell us what his name is."

Soon after that Jess and Henry heard her snoring heavily. They sat up in the dark.

"Mustn't we surely run away?" whispered Jess in Henry's ear.

"Yes!" whispered Henry. "Take only what we need most. We must be far off before morning, or they will catch us."

Jess sat still for a moment, thinking, for every motion she made must count.

"I will take both loaves of bread," she thought, "and Violet's little workbag. Henry has his knife. And all Father's money is in my pocket." She drew it out and counted it in the dark, squinting her eyes in the faint light of the moon. It amounted to nearly four dollars.

"You'll have to carry Benny until he wakes up," whispered Jess. "If we wake him up here, he might cry."

She touched Violet as she spoke.

"Sh! Violet! Come! We're going to run away," she whispered.

The little girl made no sound. She sat up obediently and tried to make out the dim shadow of her sister.

"What shall I do?" she said, light as a breath.

"Carry this," said Jess, handing her the work bag and a box of matches.

Jess tiptoed over to the tin box on the table, drew out the two loaves of bread, and slipped them into the laundry bag. She peered around the room for the last time, and then dropped two small clean towels and a cake of soap into the bag.

"All right. Pick him up," she said to Henry.

Henry bent over the sleeping child and lifted him carefully. Jess took the laundry bag, turned the doorknob ever so softly, opened the door ever so slowly, and they tiptoed out in a ghostly procession.

Jess shut the door with as much care as she had opened it, listened to the bakeshop woman's heavy snoring for a moment, and then they turned and picked their way without a sound to the country road.

"She may wake up before morning, you know," whispered Henry. "We must do our fastest walking before then. If we can only get to another town before they find out we're gone, they won't know which way to go."

Jess agreed, and they all walked briskly along in the faint moonlight.

"How far can you carry Benny?" asked Violet.

"Oh, at least a mile," said Henry confidently, although his arms were beginning to ache. Benny was five years old, and he was a fat, healthy boy as well.

"I think we could all walk faster if we woke him up," said Jess decidedly. "We could each take his hand and almost carry him along."

Henry knelt by the roadside and set the little fellow against his knee.

"Come, Benny, you must wake up now and walk!" said Jess coaxingly.

"Go away!" Benny mumbled with his eyes shut, trying to lie down again.

"Let me try," Violet offered softly.

"Say, Benny, you know little Cinnamon Bear ran away to find a nice warm bed for the winter? Now, you play your Cinnamon, and Henry and Jess will help you along, and we'll find a bed."

Violet's little plan worked. Benny was never too cross to listen to the wonderful stories his sister Violet could tell about Cinnamon Bear. He stood up bravely and marched along, yawning, while his big brother and sister almost swung him between them.

Not a soul passed them on the country road. All the houses they saw were dark and still. And when the first faint streaks of morning light showed in the sky, all four children were almost staggering with sleep.

"I must go to sleep, Henry," murmured Jess at last. Little Benny was asleep already, and Henry was carrying him again.

"The first place we come to, then," painted Henry.

Violet said nothing, but she kept her eyes open.

Finally she caught Henry's sleeve. "Couldn't we make that haystack?" she asked, pointing across a newly mown field.

"Indeed we could," said Henry thankfully. "What a big, enormous one it is! I was too sleepy to see it, I guess."

"And see how far away from the farmhouse and barn it is, too!" echoed Jess.

The sight gave them new courage. They climbed over two stone walls, got across a brook somehow with the heavy child, and arrived at the haystack.

Henry laid his brother down and stretched his aching arms, while Jess began to burrow into the haystack. Violet, after a moment of watching her, did the same.

"Here's his nest," said Jess sleepily, taking her head out of the deep round hole she had made. Henry lifted the child into the opening and was pleased to see that he curled up instantly, smiling in his sleep.

Jess pulled wisps of hay over the opening so that it was absolutely invisible, and then proceeded to dig out a similar burrow for herself.

"We can stay here just—as long—as we like, can't we, Henry?" she murmured, digging with her eyes shut.

"We sure can," replied Henry. "You're an old brick, Jess. Get in, and I'll pull the hay over the hole."

Violet was already curled up in her nest, which was hidden so completely that Henry spoke to her to see if she was there. Then he wriggled himself backward into the haycock without stopping to hollow it out, pulled a handful of hay over his head, and laid his head on his arm.

Just as he did so he heard a heavy voice say, "Now, then, lass, git along!" Then he heard the rumble of a milk wagon coming down a near-by lane, and he realized thankfully that they had hidden themselves just before the first farmer in the neighborhood had set off toward Middlesex with his milk cans.

"He will say he didn't meet us coming this way," thought Henry, "so they will hunt for us the other way. And that will give us time to cover a lot more ground."

He dropped asleep just as the roosters all over the valley began to answer each other.

THE SECOND NIGHT

The roosters crowed and the hens clucked; the farmer's wife began to get breakfast, and the four children slept on. Dinner time came and went, and still they slept, for it must be remembered that they had been awake and walking during the whole night. In fact, it was nearly seven o'clock in the evening when they awoke. Luckily, all the others awoke before Benny.

"Can you hear me, Jess?" said Henry, speaking very low through the wall of hay.

"Yes," answered Jess softly. "Let's make one big room for our nests."

No sooner said than done. The boy and girl worked quickly and quietly until they could see each other. They pressed the hay back firmly until they had made their way into Violet's little room. And then she in turn groped until she found Benny.

"Hello, little Cinnamon!" whispered Violet playfully.

And Benny at once made up his mind to laugh instead of cry. But laughing out loud was almost as bad, so Henry took his little brother on the hay beside him and talked to him seriously.

"You're old enough now, Benny, to understand what I say to you. Now, listen! When I tell you to keep still after this, that means you're to stop crying if you're crying, or stop laughing if you're laughing, and be just as still as you possibly can. If you don't mind, you will be in danger. Do you understand?"

"Don't I have to mind Jess and Violet too?" asked Benny.

"Absolutely!" said Henry. "You have to mind us all, every one of us!"

Benny thought a minute. "Can't I ask for what I want any more?" he said.

"Indeed you can!" cried Jess and Henry together. "What is it you want?"

"I'm awfully hungry," said Benny anxiously.

Henry's brow cleared. "Good old Benny," he said. "We're just going to have supper—or is it breakfast?"

Jess drew out the fragrant loaf of bread. She cut it with Henry's jackknife into four quarters, and she and Henry took the two crusty ends themselves.

"That's because we have to be the strongest, and crusts make you strong," explained Jess.

Violet looked at her older sister. She thought she knew why Jess took the crust, but she did not speak.

"We will stay here till dark, and then we'll go on with our journey," said Henry cheerfully.

"I want a drink," announced Benny.

"A drink you shall have," Henry promised, "but you'll have to wait till it's really dark. If we should creep out to the brook now, and any one saw us—" He did not finish his sentence, but Benny realized that he must wait.

He was much refreshed from his long sleep, and felt very lively. Violet had all she could do to keep him amused, even with Cinnamon Bear and his five brothers.

At last Henry peeped out. It was after nine o'clock. There were lights in the farmhouse still, but they were all upstairs.

"We can at least get a drink now," he said. And the children crept quietly to the noisy little brook not far from the haystack.

"Cup," said Benny.

"No, you'll have to lie down and drink with your mouth," Jess explained. And so they did. Never did water taste so cool and delicious as it did that night to the thirsty children.

When they had finished drinking they jumped the brook, ran quickly over the fields to the wall, and once more found themselves on the road.

"If we meet any one," said Jess, "we must all crouch behind bushes until he has gone by."

They walked along in the darkness with light hearts. They were no longer tired or hungry. Their one thought was to get away from their grandfather, if possible.

"If we can find a big town," said Violet, "won't it be better to stay in than a little town?"

"Why?" asked Henry, puffing up the hill.

"Well, you see, there are so many people in a big town, nobody will notice us—"

"And in a little village everyone would be talking about us," finished Henry admiringly. "You've got brains, Violet!"

He had hardly said this, when a wagon was heard behind them in the distance. It was coming from Middlesex. Without a word, the four children sank down behind the bushes like frightened rabbits. They could plainly hear their hearts beat. The horse trotted nearer, and then began to walk up the hill.

"If we hear nothing in Townsend," they heard a man say, "we have plainly done our duty."

It was the baker's voice!

"More than our duty," said the baker's wife, "tiring out a horse with going a full day, from morning until night!"

There was silence as the horse pulled the creaky wagon.

"At least we will go on to Townsend tonight," continued the baker, "and tell them to watch out. We need not go to Intervale, for they never could walk so far."

"We are well rid of them, I should say," replied his wife. "They may not have come this way. The milkman did not see them, did he?"

The baker's reply was lost, for the horse had reached the hilltop, where he broke into a canter.

It was some minutes before the children dared to creep out of the bushes again.

"One thing is for sure," said Henry, when he got his breath. "We will not go to Townsend."

"And we will go to Intervale," said Jess.

With a definite goal in mind at last, the children set out again with a better spirit. They walked until two o'clock in the morning, stopping often this time to rest and to drink from the horses' watering troughs. And then they came upon a fork in the road with a white signpost shining in the moonlight.

"Townsend, four miles; Intervale, six miles," read Henry aloud. "Does one feel able to walk six more miles?"

He grinned. No one had the least idea how far they had already walked.

"We'll go that way at least," said Jess finally.

"That we will," agreed Henry, picking up his brother for a change, and carrying him "pig-back."

Violet went ahead. The new road was a pleasant woody one, with grass growing in the middle. The children could not see the grass, but they could feel it as they walked. "Not many people pass this way, I guess," remarked Violet. Just then she caught her toe in something and almost fell, but Jess caught her.

The two girls stooped down to examine the obstruction.

"Hay!" said Jess.

"Hay!" repeated Violet.

"Hey!" cried Henry, coming up. "What did you say?"

"It must have fallen off somebody's load," said Jess.

"We'll take it with us," Henry decided wisely. "Load on all you can carry, Jess."

"For Benny," thought Violet to herself. So the odd little party trudged on for nearly three hours, laden with hay, until they found that the road ended in a cart path through the woods.

"Oh, dear!" exclaimed Jess, almost ready to cry with disappointment.

"What's the matter?" demanded Henry in astonishment. "Isn't the woods a good place to sleep? We can't sleep on the road, you know."

"It does seem nice and far away from people," admitted Jess, "and it's almost morning."

As they stood still at the entrance to the woods, they heard the rumble of a train. It roared down the valley at a great rate and passed them on the other side of the woods, thundering along toward the city.

"Never mind the train, either," remarked Henry. "It isn't so awfully near; and even if it were, it couldn't see us."

He set his brother down and peered into the woods. It was very warm.

"Lizzen!" said Benny.

"Listen!" echoed Violet.

"More water!" Benny cried, catching his big brother by the hand.

"It is only another brook," said Henry with a thankful heart. "He wants a drink." The trickle of water sounded very pleasant to all the children as they lay down once more to drink.

Benny was too sleepy to eat. Jess quickly found a dry spot thick with moss between two stones. Upon this moss the three older children spread the hay in the shape of an oval bed. Benny tumbled into it with a great sigh of satisfaction, while his sisters tucked the hay around him.

"Pine needles up here, Jess," called Henry from the slope. Each of them quickly scraped together a fragrant pile for a pillow and once more lay down to sleep, with hardly a thought of fear.

"I only hope we won't have a thunderstorm," said Jess to herself, as she shut her tired eyes.

And she did not open them for a long time, although the dark gray clouds piled higher and more thickly over the sleeping children.

SHELTER

When Jess opened her eyes it must have been about ten o'clock in the morning. She sat up and looked all around her. She could dimly see the opening where they had come into the woods. She looked around to see that her family was still safe. Then she looked up at the sky. At first she thought it must still be night, and then she realized that the darkness was caused by an approaching storm.

"Whatever, whatever shall we do now?" demanded Jess of the air.

She got up and looked in every direction for shelter. She even walked quite a little way into the woods, and down a hill. And there she stood, not knowing what to do next.

"I shall have to wake Henry up," she said at last. "Only how I hate to!"

As she spoke she glanced into the forest, and her feet felt as if they were nailed to the ground. She could not stir. Faintly outlined among the trees, Jess saw an old freight or box car. Her first thought was one of fear; her second, hope for shelter. As she thought of shelter, her feet moved, and she stumbled toward it.

It really was a freight car. She felt it. It stood on rusty broken rails which were nearly covered with dead leaves. Then the thunder cracked overhead. Jess came to her usual senses and started back for Henry, flying like the wind. He was awake, looking anxiously overhead. He had not noticed that Jess was missing.

"Come!" painted Jess. "I've found a place! Hurry! hurry!"

Henry did not stop to ask questions. He picked up Benny, telling

Violet to gather up the hay. And then they ran headlong through the thick underbrush in Jess' wake, seeing their way only too well by the sharp flashes of lightning.

"It's beginning to sprinkle!" gasped Henry.

"We'll get there, all right," Jess shouted back. "It's not far. Be all ready to help me open the door when we get there!"

By sheer good fortune a big tree stump stood under the door of the freight car, or the children never could have opened it. As it was, Jess sprang on the stump and Henry, pausing to lay Benny down, did likewise. Together they rolled back the heavy door about a foot.

"That's enough," painted Jess. "I'll get in, and you hand Benny up to me."

"No," said Henry quietly. "I must see first if anyone is in there."

"It will rain!" protested Jess. "Nothing will hurt me."

But she knew it was useless to argue with Henry, so she hastily groped in the bag for the matches and handed them to her brother. It must be confessed that Jess held her breath while Henry struck one and peered about inside the car.

"All's well!" he reported. "Come in, everybody!"

Violet passed the hay up to her brother, and crawled in herself. Then Jess handed Benny up like a package of groceries and, taking one last look at the angry sky and waving trees, she climbed in after him.

The two children managed to roll the door back so that the crack was completely closed before the storm broke. But at that very instant it broke with a vengeance. It seemed to the children that the sky would split, so sharp were the cracks of thunder. But not a drop of rain reached them in their roomy retreat. They could see nothing at all, for the freight car was tightly made, and all outside was nearly as black as night. Through it all, Benny slept on.

Presently the thunder grew fainter, and rumbled away down the valley, and the rain spent itself. Only the drip from the trees on the top of the car could be heard. Then Henry ventured to open the door.

He knelt on his hands and knees and thrust his head out.

The warm sunlight was filtering through the trees, making golden pools of light here and there. The beautiful trees, pines and white birches and oaks, grew thickly around and the ground was carpeted with flowers and wonderful ferns more than a yard high. But most miraculous of all was a miniature waterfall, small but perfect, where the same little brown brook fell gracefully over some ledges, and danced away down the glen.

In an instant Jess and Violet were looking over Henry's shoulder at the pretty sight.

"How different everything looks with the sun shining!" exclaimed Jess. "Things will soon be dry at this rate."

"It must be about noon," observed Henry, looking at the sun. And as he spoke the faint echo of mill bells in the distance was heard.

"Henry!" said Jess sharply. "Let's live here!"

"Live here?" repeated Henry dully.

"Yes! Why not?" replied Jess. "Nobody uses this car, and it's dry and warm. We're quite far away. And yet we are near enough to a town so we can buy things."

"And we're near water," added Violet.

Jess hugged her sister. "So we are, little mouse," she said—"the most important thing of all."

"But—" began Henry.

"Please, Henry," said Jess excitedly. "I could make this old freight car into the dearest little house, with beds, and chairs, and a table—and dishes—"

"I'd like to live here, too," said a determined little voice from the corner, "but I don't want to, unless—"

"Unless what?" asked Henry, panic-stricken.

"Unless I can have my dinner," Benny finished anxiously.

"We'll have something to eat right away, old fellow," said Henry, thankful it was no worse. For he himself was beginning to see what a cozy home the car really would make.

Jess cut the last loaf of bread into four pieces, but alas! It was very dry. The children were so hungry that they tore it with their teeth like little dogs, but Benny was nearly crying. He did not actually cry, however, for just at the crucial moment Violet started a funny story about Cinnamon Bear eating bread crusts out of the ash can.

"He ought to have milk," said Jess quietly to Henry.

"He shall have milk," replied Henry. "I'll go down the railroad track to the town and get some."

Jess counted out a dollar in ten dimes and handed it to Henry. "By the time our four dollars are gone, you will have some work to do," she said.

All the same Henry did not like to begin his trip. "How I hate to leave you alone, Jess!" he said miserably.

"Oh, don't you worry," began Jess lightly. "We'll have a surprise for you when you come back. You just wait and see!" And she nodded her head wisely as Henry walked slowly off through the woods.

The moment he was out of sight she turned to Benny and Violet. "Now, children," she said, "what do you think we're going to do? Do you know what I saw over in the sunny part of the woods? I saw some blueberries!"

"Oh, oh!" cried Benny, who knew what blueberries were. "Can't we have some blueberries and milk?"

"We certainly—" began Jess. But the sentence never was finished, for a sharp crackle of dry leaves was heard. Something was moving in the woods.

A NEW HOME

"Keep still!" whispered Jess.

Benny obeyed. The three children were as motionless as stone images, huddled inside the freight car. Jess opened her mouth in order to breathe at all, her heart was thumping so wildly. She watched like a cat through the open door, in the direction of the rustling noise. And in a moment the trembling bushes parted, and out crawled a dog. He was an Airedale and was pulling himself along on three legs, whimpering softly.

Jess drew a long breath of relief, and said to the children, "It's all right. Only a dog. But he seems to be hurt."

At the sound of her voice the dog lifted his eyes and wagged his tail feebly. He held up his front foot.

"Poor doggie," murmured Jess soothingly, as she clambered out of the car. "Let Jess see your poor lame foot." She approached the dog carefully, for she remembered that her mother had always told her never to touch a strange dog unless he wagged his tail.

But this dog's tail was wagging, certainly, so Jess bent over without fear to look at the paw. An exclamation of pity escaped her when she saw it, for a stiff, sharp thorn had been driven completely through one of the cushions of the dog's foot, and around it the blood had dried.

"I guess I can fix that," said Jess briskly. "But taking the thorn out is going to hurt you, old fellow."

The dog looked up at her as she laid his paw down, and licked her hand.

"Come here, Violet and Benny," directed Jess.

She took the animal gently in her lap and turned him on his side. She patted his head and stroked his nose with one finger, and offered him the rest of her breadcrust, which she had put in her apron pocket. The dog snapped it up as if he were nearly starving. Then she held the soft paw firmly with her left hand, and pulled steadily on the thorn with her right hand. The dog did not utter a sound. He lay motionless in her lap, until the thorn suddenly let go and lay in Jess' hand.

"Good, good!" cried Violet.

"Wet my handkerchief," Jess ordered briskly.

Violet did so, dipping it in the running brook. Jess wrapped the cool, wet folds around the hot paw, and gently squeezed it against the wound, the dog meanwhile trying to lick her hands.

"We'll surprise Henry, won't we?" laughed Benny delightedly. "Now we got a dog!"

"To be sure," said Jess, struck with the thought, "but that isn't what I intended for a surprise. You know I was intending to get a lot of blueberries, and maybe find some old dishes in a dump or something—"

"Can't we look while you hold the dog?" asked Violet anxiously.

"Of course you can, Pet!" said Jess. "Look over there by those rocks."

Benny and Violet scrambled through the underbrush to the place Jess pointed out, and investigated. But they did not hunt long, for the blueberries were so thick that the bushes almost bent over with their weight.

"O Jessy," screamed Benny, "you never saw so many in your life! What'll we pick 'em into?"

"Come and get a clean towel," said Jess, who noticed that Benny was already "picking into" his own mouth.

"But that's just as well," she thought. "Because he won't get so hungry waiting for the milk." She watched the two children a moment as they dropped handfuls of the bluish globes on the towel. Then she carefully got up with her little patient and went over and sat down in the center of the patch. The berries were so thick she did not have to change her position before the towel held over a quart.

"Oh, dear," sighed Jess. "I wish I could hunt for some dishes, so we could have blueberries and milk."

"Never mind tonight," said Violet. "We can just eat a handful of berries and then take a drink of milk, when Henry comes."

But it was even better than that, for when Henry came he had two bottles of milk under one arm, a huge loaf of brown bread under the other, and some golden cheese in waxed paper in his pocket.

But you should have seen Henry stare when he saw what Jess was holding!

"Where in the world—" began the boy.

"He came to us," volunteered Benny. "He came as a surprise for you. And he's a nice doggie."

Henry knelt down to look at the visitor, who wagged his tail. "It wouldn't be a bad thing to have a watchdog," said Henry. "I worried about you all the time I was gone."

"Did you bring some milk?" inquired Benny, trying to be polite, but looking at the bottles with longing eyes.

"Bless his heart!" said Jess, struggling to her feet with the dog. "We'll have dinner right away—or is it supper?"

"Call it supper," suggested Henry, "for it's the last thing we'll have to eat today."

"And then tomorrow we'll start having three meals every day," laughed Jess.

It was certainly a queer meal, whatever it was. Jess, who liked above all things to be orderly, spread out the big gray laundry bag on the pine needles for a tablecloth. The brown loaf was cut by a very excited little hostess into five thick squares; the cheese into four.

"Dogs don't eat cheese," Benny remarked cheerfully. The poor little fellow was glad of it, too, for he was very hungry. He could hardly wait for Jess to set the milk bottles in the center of the table and heap the blueberries in four little mounds, one at each place.

"I'm sorry we don't have cups," Jess remarked. "We'll just have to drink out of the same bottle."

"No, we won't," said Henry. "We'll drink half of each bottle, so that will make at least two things to drink out of."

"Good for you, Henry," said Jess, much relieved. "You and Benny use one, and Violet and I will use the other."

So the meal began. "Look, Benny," directed Henry. "Eat a handful of blueberries, then take a bite of brown bread, then a nibble of cheese. Now, a drink of milk!"

"It's good! It's good!" mumbled Benny to himself all through the meal.

You must not imagine that the poor wandering dog was neglected, for Jess fed him gently, as he lay in her lap, poking morsels of bread into his mouth and pouring milk into her own hand for him to lap up.

When the meal was over, and exactly half of each bottle of milk remained, Jess said, "We are going to sleep on beds tonight, and just as soon as we get our beds made, we are all going to be washed."

"That'll be fun, Benny," added Violet. "We'll wash our paws in the brook just the way Cinnamon does."

"First, let's gather armfuls of dry pine needles," ordered Jess. "Get those on top that have been lying in the sunshine." Jess laid the dog down on a bed of moss as she spoke, and started energetically to scoop up piles of the fragrant needles. Soon a pile as high as her head stood just under the freight-car door.

"I think we have enough," she said at last. Taking the scissors from Violet's workbag, she cut the laundry bag carefully into two pieces, saving the cord for a clothesline. One of the big squares was laid across Benny's hay and tucked under. That was the softest bed of all. Violet's apron and her own, she cut off at the belt.

"I'll sleep next to Benny," said Henry, "with my head up by the door. Then I can hear what is going on." A big pile of pine needles was loaded into the freight car for Henry's bed, and covered with the other half of the laundry bag.

The remainder of the needles Jess piled into the farthest corner of the car for herself and Violet. "We'll all sleep on one side, so we can call it the bedroom."

"What'll be on the other side?" inquired Benny.

"The other side?" repeated Jess. "Let me think! I guess that'll be the sitting room, and perhaps some of the time the kitchen."

"On rainy days, maybe the dining room," added Henry with a wink.

"Couldn't it be the parlor?" begged Benny.

"Certainly, the parlor! We forgot that," agreed Jess, returning the wink. She was covering the last two soft beds with the two aprons. "The tops of these aprons are washcloths," she said severely. Then armed with the big cake of soap she led the way to the brook. The dog watched them anxiously, but when Jess said, "Lie still," he obeyed. From the moment Jess drew the thorn from his foot he was her dog, to obey her slightest command and to follow her wherever she went.

The clean cool brook was delightful even to Benny. The children rolled up their sleeves and plunged their dusty arms into its waters, quarreling good-naturedly over the soap, and lathering their stained faces and necks with it. When they were well rinsed with clear water they dried themselves with the towel. Then Jess washed bath towels nicely with soap, rinsed them, and hung them on the clothesline of tape, which she had stretched between two slender birch trees. They flapped lazily in the wind.

"Looks like home already, Jess," said Henry, smiling at the washing.

The tired children clambered into the "bedroom," Jess coming last with the wounded dog.

"We'll have to leave the door open, it's so hot," said Henry, lying down with a tired sigh.

And in less than ten minutes they were fast asleep, dog and all—asleep at six o'clock, asleep without naming the dog, without locking the door, without fear, for this was the first night in four that they had been able to go to sleep at night, as children should.

HOUSEKEEPING

The next morning Jess was up before the others, as was fitting for a little housekeeper. That is, she was first if we except the dog, who had opened one eye instantly every time his little mistress stirred in her sleep. He sat watching gravely in the door of the car as Jess descended to get breakfast. She walked from the little waterfall quite a distance down the brook, looking at it with critical eyes.

"This will be the well," she said to herself, regarding a small but deep and quiet basin just below the falls. Below that she found a larger basin, lined with gravel, with flat stones surrounding it.

"This will be the washtub," she decided. "And now I must go back to the refrigerator." This was the strangest spot of all, for behind the little waterfall was a small quiet pool in which Jess had set the milk bottles the night before. Not a drop of water could get in, but all night long the cool running water had surrounded the bottles. They were now fairly icy to the touch. Jess smiled as she drew them out.

"Is it good?" asked Benny's voice. There he sat in the door of the car, swinging his legs, his arm around the shaggy dog.

"It's delicious!" declared Jess. "Cold as ice." She climbed up beside him as she spoke, bringing the breakfast with her. The other two children sat up and looked at it.

"Today, Jess," began Henry, "I will go back to town and try to get a job mowing lawns or something. Then we can afford to have something besides milk for breakfast."

Milk suited Benny very well, however, so the older children allowed him to drink rather more than his share. Henry did not waste any time talking. He brushed his hair as well as he could without a brush, rolled down his sleeves, and started for town with the second dollar.

"Glad you've got a dog, Jess," he called back, as he waved his straw hat.

The children watched him disappear around the curve and then turned to Jess expectantly. They were not mistaken. Jess had a plan.

"We'll explore," she began mysteriously. "We'll begin here at the car, and hunt all over these woods until we find a dump!"

"What's a dump?" inquired Benny.

"O Benny!" answered Violet. "You know what a dump is. All old bottles and papers and broken dishes."

"And wheels?" asked Benny interestedly. "Will there be any old wheels?"

"Yes, maybe," assented Violet. "But cups, Benny! Think of drinking milk out of a cup again!"

"Oh, yes," said Benny, politely. But it was clear that his mind was centered on wheels rather than cups.

The exploring party started slowly down the rusty track, with the dog hopping happily on three legs. The fourth paw, nicely bandaged with Jess' handkerchief, he held up out of harm's way.

"I think this is a spur track," said Jess. "They built it in here so they could load wood on the cars, and then when they had cut all the wood they didn't need the track any more."

This explanation seemed very likely, for here and there were stumps of trees and decaying chips. Violet took note of these chips, and remembered them some days later. In fact, both girls kept their eyes open, and pointed out things of interest to each other.

"Remember these logs, Violet, if we should ever need any," said Jess pointing.

"Blackberry blossoms!" returned Violet briefly, turning one over gently with her foot.

"Big flat stones!" remarked Jess, later on, as they came upon a great heap of them.

Here the track came out into the open sunshine, and broken pieces of rail showed clearly where it had joined the main track at some time in the past. And here from the top of the wooded hill the children could plainly see the city in the valley. They walked along the track, picking out a church steeple here and there, forgetting for a moment the object of their search.

"There's a wheel!" Benny cried triumphantly from behind.

The girls looked down, and with a glad cry of surprise Jess recognized a dump at the foot of the hill. They found it not composed entirely of ashes and tin cans, either, although both of these were there in great profusion. It was a royal dump, containing both cups and wheels.

"O Benny!" cried Jess, "if it hadn't been for you!" She hugged him, wheel and all, and began turning over the rubbish with great delight.

"Here's a white pitcher, Jess," Violet called, holding up a perfect specimen with a tiny chip in its nose.

"Here's a big white cup," said Jess delightedly, laying it aside.

"Want a teapot, Jessy?" inquired Benny, offering her an enormous blue enameled affair without a handle.

"Yes, indeed!" cried Jess. "We can use that for water. I've found two cups and a bowl already. And Violet, we ought to be looking for spoons, too."

Violet pointed without speaking to her little pile of treasures. There were five iron spoons covered with rust.

"Wonderful!" pronounced Jess with rapture. Indeed, it is doubtful if collectors of rare and beautiful bits of porcelain ever enjoyed a search as much as did these adventurers in the dump heap.

Benny actually found four wheels, exactly alike, probably from the same cart, and insisted upon carrying them back. To please him, Jess allowed him to add them to the growing pile.

"Here's a big iron kettle," observed Violet. "But we won't really cook with a fire, will we, Jess?"

"We'll take it back, though," replied Jess with a knowing look. "We can pile lots of dishes in it."

They could, and did, but not until after Benny had discovered his beloved "pink cup." It was a tea-party cup of bright rose-color with a wreath of gorgeous roses on it, and a little shepherdess giving her lamb a drink from a pale blue brook. It had a perfectly good handle, gold into the bargain. Its only flaw was a dangerous crack through the lamb's nose and front feet. Jess made a cushion for it out of grass and laid it on top of the kettle full of treasures. All the things, even the wheels, were laid on a wide board which the two girls carried between them.

Benny discovered his beloved "pink cup"

Can you imagine the dishwashing when the gay party returned to the freight car? Children do not usually care for dishwashing. But never did a little boy hand dishes to his sister so carefully as Benny did. On their hands and knees beside the clear, cool little "washtub," the three children soaped and rinsed and dried their precious store of dishes. Jess scoured the rust from the spoons with sand. "There!" she said, drying the last polished spoon. The children sat back and looked admiringly at their own handiwork. But they did not look long. There was too much to be done.

"Jess," exclaimed Violet, "I'll tell you!" Violet seldom spoke so excitedly. Even Benny turned around and looked at her.

"Come and see what I noticed inside the car last night!"

Both children followed her, and peered in at the door.

"See, on the wall, right over on the other door, Jess." Now, all Jess could see were two thick chunks of wood nailed securely to the closed door opposite the open one. But she whirled around and around as fast as she could, clapping her hands. When she could get her breath, however, she skipped over to the board they had carried, dusted it nicely, and laid it carefully across the two wooden projections. It was a perfect shelf.

"There!" said Jess.

The children could hardly wait to arrange the shining new dishes on the shelf. Violet quietly gathered some feathery white flowers, a daisy or two, and some maidenhair ferns, which she arranged in a glass vase filled with water from the "well." This she put in the middle, with the broken edge hidden.

"There!" said Jess.

"You said 'there' three times, Jessy," remarked Benny, contentedly.

"So I did," replied Jess laughing, "but I'm going to say it again." She pointed and said, "There!"

Henry was coming up the path.

EARNING A LIVING

Henry had all sorts of packages under his arm and in his pockets. But he wouldn't open them or tell a thing about his adventures until dinner was ready, he said. "Jess, you're a wonder!" he exclaimed when he saw the dishes and the shelf.

The big kettle was selected, and they all began to pick blueberries as fast as they could, telling Henry meanwhile all about the wonderful dump. At last the tablecloth was spread and Henry unwrapped his parcels before the whole excited family.

"I bought some more brown bread," he said, producing the loaves, "and some more milk—in the same little store where I went yesterday. It's kept by a little old man, and it's called a Delicatessen Shop. He has everything in his store to eat. I bought some dried beef because we can eat it with our fingers. And I bought a big bone for the dog."

"His name is Watch," Jess interrupted.

"All right," said Henry, accepting the name. "I bought a bone for Watch."

Watch fell on the bone as if he were famished, which indeed he nearly was.

It was a rapturous moment when Jess poured the yellow milk into four cups or bowls, and each child proceeded to crumble the brown bread into it with a liberal scattering of blueberries. And then when they ate it with spoons! Nobody was able to speak a word for several minutes.

Then Henry began slowly to tell his tale.

"I earned a dollar just this morning," he began proudly. "I walked along the first shady street I came to—nice houses, you know. And there was a fellow out mowing his own lawn. He's a nice fellow, too, I can tell you—a young doctor." Henry paused to chew blissfully.

"He was pretty hot," Henry went on. "And just as I came to the gate, his telephone rang. I heard it, and called after him and asked if he didn't want me to finish up."

"And he said he did!" cried Jess.

"Yes. He said, 'For goodness' sake, yes!'" Henry answered smiling. "You see, he wasn't used to it. So I mowed the lawn and trimmed the edges, and he said he never had a boy trim it as well as I did. And then he asked me if I wanted a steady job."

"O Henry!" cried Violet and Jess together.

"I told him I did, so he said to come back this afternoon any time I wanted, or tomorrow—he said he didn't care just when—any time."

Henry gave his cup a last polish with his spoon and set it down dreamily. "It's a pretty house," he went on, "and there's a big garden behind it—vegetable garden. And an orchard behind that—cherry orchard. You ought to see the cherry trees! Well, when I was trimming the edges near the kitchen door, the cook came and watched me. She's a fat Irish Woman." Henry laughed at the recollection.

"She asked me if I liked cookies. Oh, if you had smelled them baking you'd have died laughing, Benny. Dee-licious! So I said I did, and she passed me one, and when she went back I put it in my pocket."

"Did she see you?" asked Jess anxiously.

"Oh, no," said Henry confidently. "For I carefully chewed away for a long time on nothing at all."

Benny began to look fixedly at Henry's pocket. It certainly was still rather bulgy.

"When I went, the doctor paid me a dollar, and the cook gave me this bag."

Henry grinned as he tossed the paper bag to Jess. Inside were twelve ginger cookies with scalloped edges, smelling faintly of cinnamon and sugar.

"I'm going to keep track of everything I earn and spend," said Henry, watching Jess as she handed around the cookies with reverence.

"How are you going to write without a pencil?" asked Jess.

"There are pieces of tailor's chalk in my work bag," said Violet.

Henry gave his younger sister a gentle pat, as she returned with her work bag and fished for the chalk.

While the girls rinsed the empty dishes in the brook and stored away the food for supper, Henry was beginning his cash account on the wall of his bedroom. It was never erased, and Henry often now looks at the account with great affection.

Soon the girls came to inspect it. Meanwhile Benny looked on with great delight as Watch tried to bury his bone with only one paw to dig with.

"Earned, $1.00; Cash on hand, $3.85," read Jess aloud.

Below, he had written:

Milk	.24
Bread	.10
Bread	.20
Cheese	.10
Milk	.24

Beef	.20
Bone	.05
Cloth	.10

"Clothes!" exclaimed Violet. "What on earth?"

Henry laughed a little, and watched her face as he drew out his last package and handed it to her.

"I thought we ought to have a tablecloth," he explained. "So I got a yard at the ten-cent store—but it isn't hemmed, of course."

With a cry of delight Violet unwrapped the brown cloth with its edge of blue. Her clever fingers were already evening the two ends. She was never so happy as when with a needle.

Henry set off again with a light heart. Here was one sister curled up happily against a big tree, setting tiny stitches into a very straight hem. Here was another sister busily gathering pliant twigs into a bundle for a broom with which to sweep the stray pine needles from the house. And here was Benny, curled up sound asleep on the ground with the dog for a pillow.

It was quite late when Henry returned. In fact, it was nearly seven o'clock, although he didn't know that. Several treasures had been added in his absence. The broom stood proudly in the corner with a slim stick for a handle. The new tablecloth had been washed and was drying on the line. And Jess, who had decided to wash one garment a day, had begun with Benny's stockings. When Henry came they were being put on again with much pride by Benny himself. Violet had darned a big hole in each.

This time Henry himself could not wait to tell his sisters what he had. He passed them the package at once, with shining eyes.

"Butter!" cried Jess with a radiant face.

It was butter, cool and sweet. Nobody remembered that they had been a week without tasting either butter or meat when at last they sat down to their royal supper.

"These are trick spoons," explained Henry. "Turn them upside down, and use the handle, and they become knives."

They were knives; anyway, they were used to spread the delicious morsels of butter on the brown loaf. With dried beef, and a cookie for dessert, who could ask for better fare? Certainly not the four children, who enjoyed it more than the rarest dainties.

"I washed the doctor's automobile this afternoon," Henry related. "Then I washed both pizzas with the hose, and tomorrow I'm going to hoe in the garden. Oh, wouldn't I love to have a nice cold swim in that brook!"

Henry was hot and sticky, certainly. He looked with longing eyes at the waterfall as he finished the last crumbs of his supper.

"I wonder if we couldn't fix up a regular swimming pool," he said, half to himself.

"Of course we could," replied Violet, as if nothing were too difficult. "Jess and I know where there are big logs, and big flat stones."

"You do, hey?" said Henry, staring at his gentle little sister.

"Well, why couldn't we, Henry?" struck in Jess. "Just a little below this there is a sort of pool already, only not big enough."

"We sure could!" cried Henry. "Someday I'll stay home from work, and we'll see."

Nobody realized that Henry had been working only one day in all. Anyway it seemed as if they had always lived in the comfortable home in the freight car, with Henry plying back and forth from the city each day, bringing them new surprises.

Henry went to bed that night with a head full of plans for damming up the brook. He almost shouted when he thought suddenly of Benny's wheels. He began to plan to make a cart to carry the heavy stones to the brook. And that was when he first noticed that Watch was not asleep. He could see his eyes shining red in the darkness. It must have been around eleven o'clock.

Henry reached over and patted his rough little back. Watch licked the hand, but didn't close his eyes. Suddenly he began to growl softly.

"Sh!" said Henry to the dog. Now thoroughly startled, he sat up; Jess sat up. They did not hear a sound.

"Better shut the door," breathed Henry. Together they rolled the door very slowly and softly until it was shut.

Still they did not hear anything. But still Watch continued his uneasy growling.

Violet and Benny slumbered on. Jess and Henry sat motionless, with their hearts in their mouths.

"Supposing it was some other tramp," whispered Jess, "somebody else that wanted to sleep here!"

"Watch would bite 'em," whispered Henry briefly. Jess never knew what confidence Henry had in the faithful dog.

Then a branch cracked sharply outside, and Watch barked out loud. Jess smothered the dog instantly in her arms. But it had been a bark and it was loud, clear, and unmistakable.

"That settles it," thought Henry. "Whoever it is, knows there's someone in here." And the boy waited with the new broom in his hand, expecting every moment to see the door open from the outside.

But nothing happened. Nothing at all. The children sat in perfect silence for at least a half hour, and nothing more was heard. Watch sniffed a little when Henry finally rolled the door open again. But he then turned around three times and lay down beside Jess, apparently satisfied at last.

Taking the dog's conduct as a sure guide, Henry composed himself for sleep.

"It must have been a rabbit or something," he said to Jess.

The occupants of the freight car slept peacefully until morning.

AT HOME

Jess and Henry had a short committee meeting the next morning before the others awoke. It was agreed that nobody should be allowed to stray off into the woods alone, not even the dog. And with much mystery Henry left some orders with all of them, as to what they should build for him during the morning.

"What for?" asked Benny.

"Shan't tell, old fellow," teased Henry. "You just build it, and you'll see later."

So Henry walked briskly through the woods, feeling sure that the noise in the night had been made by a rabbit.

Having no watch, Henry made a slight mistake by appearing at the young doctor's door before eight o'clock. He was just in time to meet the doctor coming in from a night call.

If Henry had not been so eager to begin work, he would have noticed how the young man's dark eyes examined him from head to foot, even to his plastered hair, wet with brook water. It was not the doctor who directed his work, but the doctor's mother—the sweet-faced Mrs. McAllister, whose heart was centered in her son and her vegetable garden.

Her heart warmed to the boy when she saw how carefully he thinned out the carrots, which had been sadly neglected.

"I have been so busy," she declared, "that I have actually stayed awake nights worrying about these carrots. There—see that?" She pulled out a fairly good-sized carrot as she spoke. It had to come out, for it was much too near its neighbors. In fact, when Henry had thinned out half a row he had quite a little pile of edible carrots, each as large as his thumb. When Mrs. McAllister saw Henry deftly press the earth back again around the carrots which remained standing, she left him quietly with a smile. Here was a gardener whom she could trust.

Henry worked steadily in the hot sun, completing row after row of carrots, parsnips, and onions. When the mill bells rang at noon he worked on, without noticing that his employer was again watching him.

When he did at last notice her he asked her, smiling, what she wanted done with the things he had pulled up.

"Oh, throw them away," she said indifferently. "Toss them over into the orchard, and sometimes we'll burn them when they get dry."

"Do you mind if I take them myself?" asked Henry, hesitatingly.

"Oh, no," said Mrs. McAllister cordially. "Do you have chickens? That will be fine."

Henry was thankful that she went right along without waiting for an answer. But in a way he did have chickens, he thought.

"You must stop working now," she said. "Anytime you want to do something, there will be a place for you here." She gave him a dollar bill, and left the delighted boy with the piles of precious little vegetables. As long as Henry expected to return so soon, he hastily selected an orderly bunch of the largest of the carrots and the smallest of the onions. He added a few of the miniature parsnips for good measure. They looked like dolls' vegetables. When Henry walked down the drive with his "bouquet," he would have seen a face at the window if he had looked up. But he did not look up. He was too anxious to get to the little old man's shop and order his meat.

So it happened that Henry walked in upon his little family at about two o'clock with all the materials for a feast. The feast could not be made ready before night, Jess hastened to explain to Benny, who was perfectly satisfied anyway with bread and milk in his pink cup.

"Your building is done," Benny informed his brother. "I builded lots of it."

"He really did," agreed Violet, leading the way to the sunny open spot a trifle behind the house. The "building" was a fireplace. With an enormous amount of labor, the children had made quite a hollow at the base of a rock. This was lined completely with flat stones. More flat stones had been set on end to keep out the wind. On top of the stones lay the most wonderful collection of firewood that you can imagine, all ready to light. There were chips and bits of crumpled paper, pine cones, and dry twigs. Beside the big rock was a woodpile. The children had apparently been working like beavers all morning. Jess had found a heavy wire in the dump, and had fastened it between two trees. On the wire the kettle swung merrily.

"Fine! Fine!" shouted Henry when he saw it. "I couldn't have done it so well myself." And he honestly believed it.

"We have dinner at night here," observed Jess impressively. "What did you buy?"

When the girls saw the tiny vegetables they began with cries of delight to cut them from their stalks with Henry's knife and a broken paring knife. They scrubbed them in the "washtub," filled the kettle half full of water from the "well," and proceeded in great excitement to cut the raw meat into cubes. When this had been dropped into the kettle, Henry lit the fire. It burned frantically, as if it were trying to encourage the stew to do its best. Violet laid the tin plate over the top for a cover, and they all stood by to hear the first bubble. Soon the savory stuff in the kettle began to boil in good earnest. Watch sat down gravely near it, and gave an approving sniff at intervals.

"Keep it boiling," advised Henry as he departed again. "When I come home tonight I'll bring some salt. And for mercy's sake, don't get on fire."

Violet pointed silently at the big teapot. The little girl had filled it with water in case of an emergency. "That's if Benny gets on fire," she explained—"or Watch."

Henry laughed and went on his way happily enough. He wished he might share the delightful task of keeping the fire going and sniffing the stew, but when he found out about his afternoon's duties, he changed his mind abruptly.

"Think you can clean up this garage?" asked Dr. McAllister quizzically when he appeared.

Henry flashed a look around the place, and met the young man's eyes with a smile. It did need cleaning rather badly. When its owner purred out in his high-powered little car, Henry drew a long breath and began in earnest. He opened all the chests of drawers to begin with. Then he arranged all the tools in the largest deep drawer, and with a long-handled brush and a can of black paint that was nearly dry, he labeled the drawer TOOLS with neat lettering. Another drawer he lettered NAILS, and assorted its contents into a few of the many boxes that were lying around. He folded up the robes he found, swept off the shelves and arranged the oil cans in orderly ranks, sorted out innumerable pairs of gloves, and then swept the floor. He washed the cement floor with the hose, and while waiting for it to dry he rinsed his brushes in turpentine.

To tell the truth, Henry had found a few things in the rubbish which he had stored in his own pocket. The treasure consisted in this case of a quantity of bent and rusty nails of all sizes, and a few screws and nuts.

When Dr. McAllister returned at six o'clock he found Henry corking up the turpentine and arranging the brushes on the shelf.

"My word!" he exclaimed, staring at his garage with his mouth open. Then he threw back his head and laughed till his mother came down the walk to see what the matter was.

"Look at my gloves, Mother," he said, wiping his eyes. "All matted up. They never met each other before, that I remember."

Mrs. McAllister looked the garage over, and observed the newly labeled drawers. Her son opened one of them, and looked at his four hammers.

"My tack hammer, Mother," he said, "your tack hammer, and two other hammers! That last one I never expected to see again. If you can use it, you may have it, my boy."

Now, it is no exaggeration to say that at that moment if Henry had been asked what he wanted most of anything in the world he would have answered without any hesitation whatsoever, "A hammer."

He accepted it gratefully, hardly able to stand still, so anxious was he to put it into use on the hill he called home.

"Tomorrow's Sunday," said the doctor. "Shall I see you on Monday?"

"Oh, yes," replied Henry, who had lost track of the days.

"The cherries need picking," said his new friend. "We could use any number of cherry pickers, if they were as careful as you." He gave him an odd look.

"Could you?" asked Henry eagerly. "I'll surely come down."

With that, he bade his friends good-by and started for home, richer by another dollar, two doughnuts the cook had given him, a pocket full of crooked nails, and the rest of the vegetables.

When he reached his freight-car home a delicious savor greeted him.

"Onions!" he shouted, running up to the kettle. The cook stood by and took off the cover and put in the salt. It was absolutely the most tantalizing odor that Henry had ever smelled. Years afterward Jess tried to duplicate it with the same kettle, vegetables from the same garden and all stirred with the same spoon, but it didn't equal this stew in flavor.

"A ladle, as sure as I live!" gasped Henry. Jess had found a tin cup in the dump, and fastened on a wooden handle with a bit of wire. And when she ladled out four portions on four plates of all sizes, some of them tin, and laid a spoon in each, the children felt that the world held no greater riches. The tiny onions floated around like pearls; the carrots melted in your mouth; and the shreds of meat were as tender as possible from long boiling. A bit of bread in one hand helped the feast along wonderfully. The little wanderers ate until they could eat no more.

"I have time before dark to make Benny's cart," observed Henry, biting a crisp, sweet carrot.

"With my wheels?" asked Benny.

"Yes, sir, with your wheels," agreed Henry. "Only, when it's done, you'll have to cart stones in it."

"Sure," said Benny with satisfaction. "Cart stones or anything."

"We'll need it in making the dam," explained Henry for the benefit of his sisters. "Tomorrow's Sunday, so I shan't work down in the town. Do you think it's all right to build the pool on Sunday, Jess?"

"I certainly do," replied Jess with emphasis. "We're just building the dam so we can keep clean. I guess if Sunday is your only day off, it'll be alright."

Henry's conscience was set at rest as he began with great delight to hammer out his bent nails. He and Benny ran about finding pieces of wood to fasten the wheels on. A visit to the dump was necessary at last, in order to find just the right piece of timber for a tongue, but before it was too dark to see, Henry had pounded the last nail in place and trundled the flat cart back and forth just to see it go. The cart seemed valuable enough to all of them to take into the house for the night. And Henry could not afford to laugh at Benny for going to sleep with his hand upon one of his precious wheels, for he himself had tucked his new hammer under his pillow.

BUILDING THE DAM

Even a hammer makes a good pillow if one is tired enough, and the freight-car family slept until the nine-o'clock church bells began to ring faintly in the valley. There were at least a dozen churches, and their far-away bells sounded sweetly harmonious in so many different keys.

"They almost play a tune," said Violet, as she listened.

"I like music all right," replied Henry in a business-like way, "but I for one shall have to get to work."

"This will be a good day to wash all the stockings," said Jess. "We'll all be wading so much in the brook, anyway."

After breakfast the first thing Henry did was to survey, with critical eyes, the spot they had chosen for a pool. It was a hollow about three yards across. There were no stones in it at all.

"It's big enough already," remarked Henry at last, "but it hasn't enough water in it." He measured its depth with a stick. "We'll have to guess at inches," he said.

"I have a little tape measure in my work bag," ventured his sister Violet.

Henry flashed a smile at her. "Is there anything you haven't got in your work bag?" he asked her.

The children measured the wet stick carefully. The water was just ten inches deep in the deepest part.

Henry explained his plan of engineering to his sisters. "We will have to haul some big logs across this narrow part and stuff them from this end with stones and underbrush. It ought to be three feet deep before we get through."

"O Henry!" protested Jess. "Benny would get drowned."

"Drowned!" echoed Henry. "How tall do you think he is, anyhow?"

They measured the little boy and found him to be forty-two inches tall. That settled it; the pool was designed to be three feet in depth.

Luckily the largest logs were not far away; but as it was, it was a matter of great labor for the builders to drag them to the scene of operations.

"Let's get all the logs up here first," suggested Jess. "Then we can have the fun of laying them across."

The two older children dragged all the logs, while Violet and Benny attended to the stones, with the help of the cart. Occasionally Henry was called upon to assist with a heavy stone, but for the most part Benny puffed out his cheeks and heaved the stones himself. In fact, Henry decided at this point to let Benny drop them into the water as he gathered them. "Splash 'em right in, old fellow," he directed. "Only keep them in a nice straight line right across this place between these two trees. It won't make any difference how wet he gets," he added in an aside to Jess. "We can dry him in the sun."

Jess thought a little differently, although she said nothing. She took off Benny's little crinkled blouse and one pair of bloomers, and started to hang them on the line.

"Good time to wash them!" she exclaimed.

"Let me wash them," begged Violet. "You're more useful building the dam." There was wisdom in this suggestion, so Jess accepted it gratefully, and even added Henry's blouse to the laundry.

"When we finish the dam they will surely be dry," she said.

As for Henry, he was only too glad to work without it. "Makes me feel lighter," he declared.

Rare and beautiful birds came and watched the barefooted children as they scurried around, building their wall of masonry. But the children did not have any eyes for birds then. They watched with delighted eyes as each stone was added to the wall under the clear water, and it began to rise almost to the surface.

"That makes a solid foundation for the logs, you see," explained Henry with pride. "They won't be floating off downstream the minute we lay them on."

Then at last the time arrived when they were to lay the logs on.

"Let's wedge the first one between these two trees," said Jess, with a happy thought. "Then if each end of the log is on the upper side of the trees, the harder the water pounds the tighter the dam gets."

"Good work!" exclaimed Henry admiringly. "That's just what we'll do."

But the children were not at all prepared for what happened the moment the first big log was splashed into its place on top of the stone wall.

The water, defeated in its course down the rocky bed, gurgled and chased about as it met the opposing log, and found every possible hole to escape.

"Leaks," said Henry briefly, as the water began to rush around both ends and pour over the top of the log. "We'll make the logs so thick it can't get through. We'll lay three logs across, with three logs on top of them, and three more on top of that."

The children set about stubbornly to accomplish this. Violet held great sprays of fine underbrush in place until each log was laid. Wetter children never were seen. But nobody cared. They resolutely plugged the ends with more stones, more underbrush, and more logs. Each time a leak was discovered, someone dropped a stone over it. Even Benny caught the fever of conquering the mischievous water which slipped from their grasp like quicksilver.

When the three top logs were at last dropped into place, the excited children sat down to watch the pool fill. This it did slowly.

Finding no means of exit, the water was quieter. It rose steadily up the barricade of logs. It widened beautifully. Henry could not sit still. "It slopes!" he cried. "See how clear it is! And still! See how still it is!"

And then the water began to overflow the logs. It spilled over the top with a delightful curve. And on the other side it formed a second waterfall—not high and narrow and graceful like the natural fall above, but very low and wide. "Just like a regular mill dam," said Henry.

He held the measuring stick out as far as he could and plunged it into the water. It lacked an inch of being three feet deep.

"Deep enough," he declared.

In fact it looked so deep that Benny could not conceal a slight fear.

"That's the beauty of the slope," observed Jess. "Benny can wade in just as far as he wants to, and no farther. We all know what the bed of the pool is like—no holes or stones."

The girls had to leave to prepare dinner, but Henry could not be persuaded to leave the wonderful swimming pool. "I'd rather swim than eat," he said.

Luckily for the children, their supply of provisions was the largest of any day since their flight. The girls lit the fire and heated up the remainder of the stew and cut the bread. The butter, hard and cold in the refrigerator, was taken out, and four portions cut from it. The two doughnuts made four half rings for dessert.

The cooks rang the dinner bell. This was an ingenious arrangement hung on a low branch. It consisted of a piece of bent steel swung on a string. Violet hit it sharply with another piece of steel. It sounded deeply and musically through the woods, and the boys understood it and obeyed at once.

It was evident the moment they appeared that at least three of the family had been swimming. Watch shook himself violently at intervals, spattering water drops in all directions. Henry and Benny, fresh and radiant, with plastered hair and clean dry stockings and blouses, apparently liked to swim and eat, too.

"You can actually swim a few strokes in it, Jess, if you're careful," Henry said, with excusable pride, as he sat down to dinner.

Building a dam is wonderful sauce for dinner. "I think stew is much better the second day," observed Benny, eating hungrily.

There remained two more adventures for the eventful day. The girls cut their hair. Violet's dark curls came off first. "They're awfully in the way," explained Violet, "and so much trouble when you're working."

They were tangled, too, and Jess cut them off evenly by a string, with Violet's little scissors. Jess' chestnut hair was long and silky and nicely braided, but she never murmured as it came off too. The two girls ran to the brook mirror to see how they looked. The new haircut was very becoming for both.

"I like you better that way," said Henry approvingly. "Lots more sensible when you're living in the woods."

Around four o'clock the children took a long walk in the opposite direction from any of their other explorations. They were rewarded by two discoveries. One was a hollow tree literally filled with walnuts, gathered presumably by a thrifty squirrel the previous fall. The other discovery frightened them a little just at first. With bristling back and a loud bark, Watch suddenly began to rout out something in the leaves, and that something began to cackle and half run and half fly from the intruders. It was a runaway hen. The children succeeded in catching the dog and reducing him to order, although it was clear he liked very much to chase hens.

"She had some eggs, too," remarked Benny as if trying to make pleasant conversation.

Jess bent over incredulously and saw a rude nest in the moss in which there were five eggs.

"A runaway hen!" said Henry, hardly believing his eyes. "She wants to hide her nest and raise chickens."

The children had no scruples at all about taking the eggs.

"Almost a gift from heaven," said Violet, stroking one of the eggs with a delicate finger. "It wouldn't be polite to refuse them."

Scrambled eggs made a delicious supper for the children. Jess broke all the eggs into the biggest bowl and beat them vigorously with a spoon until they were light and foamy. Then she added milk and salt and delegated Violet to beat them some more while she prepared the fire. The big kettle, empty and clean, was hung over the low fire and butter was dropped in. Jess watched it anxiously, tipping the kettle slightly in all directions. When the butter had reached the exact shade of brown, Jess poured in the eggs and stirred them carefully, holding her skirts away from the fire. She was amply repaid for her care when she saw her family attack the meal. Clearly this was a feast day.

"We shall have to be satisfied tomorrow to live on bread and milk," she observed, scraping up the last delicious morsel.

But when tomorrow came they had more than bread and milk, as you will soon see.

CHERRY PICKING

Henry meditated awhile all to himself early the next morning as to whether he ought to take any one with him for the cherry picking. "He certainly said he could use more than one," he mused.

Failing to decide the question, he laid it before his sisters as they ate bread and milk for breakfast.

"I can't see any reason, except one, why we shouldn't all go," said Jess.

"What's that?" asked Henry.

"Well, you see there are four of us, and supposing grandfather is looking for us, it will be easier to find four than one."

"True," agreed Henry. "But suppose we went down the hill and through the streets two by two? And you took Watch?"

It was finally agreed that Henry and Benny would attract very little attention together; Violet and Jess would follow with the dog, who would trace Henry. And so they set out. They took down the clothesline and closed the car door. Everything instantly looked as lonesome as the heart could wish. Even the merry little brook looked deserted.

When the children arrived at the McAllister orchard they soon saw that they were not the only workers. Two hired men and the young doctor himself were carrying ladders and baskets from the barn, and the Irish cook was bringing piles of square baskets from the house—the kind that strawberries are sold in.

"The girls can pick cherries as well as I can," said Henry, introducing his sisters. "Benny ought not to climb very tall trees, but we had to bring him."

"Benny can carry the baskets, perhaps," suggested the doctor, much amused. "You see, this is a cherry blossom year, and we have to work quickly when we begin. Perhaps he could fill the small baskets from the big ones."

It was a "cherry year," certainly. There were two varieties in the orchard, the pale yellow kind with a red cheek, and the deep crimson ones which were just as red in the center as they were on the outside. The red ones were huge, bursting with juice, and the trees were laden full with the luscious fruit. Even the air was perfumed.

It was a pretty sight that the doctor finally turned his back upon when he went on his calls. Henry, slim, tanned, and graceful, picked rapidly from the tallest ladder in the largest tree. The two girls in their sensible bloomer suits could climb like cats. They leaned against the ladders easily about halfway up, their fluffy short hair gleaming in the sun. Benny trotted to and fro, waiting upon the busy pickers, his cheeks as red as the cherries themselves.

"Eat all you want," Dr. McAllister called back. They did not really obey this command, but occasionally a set of white teeth bit into one of the glorious oxhearts.

In less than an hour Benny had made five firm friends. The hired men joked with him, the cook petted him, the young doctor laughed at him delightedly, and sweet Mrs. McAllister fell in love with him. Finally he seated himself comfortably at her side under the trees and filled square boxes with great care under her direction.

"I never had such a cheerful crowd of cherry pickers before," Mrs. McAllister said at last. "I'd much rather stay out here than go into the house where it is cool."

Evidently Mary the cook felt the same way, for she kept coming to the orchard for some reason or other. When the doctor returned at lunch time his orchard was ringing with laughter, and good-natured barks from Watch who could not feel easy in his mind with his mistress so high up in a tree where he couldn't follow.

Dr. McAllister paused in the garage long enough to give a sniff to the boiling cherries in the kitchen, and then made his way to the orchard, where he received a warm welcome.

"There's no use in your going home to lunch," he smilingly observed, at the same time watching Henry's face carefully. "You can eat right here in the orchard, unless your mother will be worrying about you."

This remark met with an astounding silence. Henry was the first to collect his wits. "No, our mother is dead," he said evenly, without embarrassment.

It was the doctor who hastened to change the subject he had introduced. "I smelled something when I came in," he said to Benny.

"What did it smell like?" inquired Benny.

"It smelled like cherry slump," replied the doctor with twinkling eyes.

"Cherry what?" asked Jess, struggling down her ladder with a full basket.

"I think that's what they call it—slump," repeated Dr. McAllister. "Do you care to try it?"

At this moment Mary appeared in the orchard with an enormous tray. And at the first sight of her cookery, nobody cared the least what its name was. It was that rare combination of dumpling beaten with stoned cherries, and cooked gently in the juice of the oxheart cherries in a real "cherry year." It was steaming in the red juice, with the least suspicion of melted butter over the whole.

"Do get two more, Mary," begged Mrs. McAllister, laughing. "It tastes so much better under the cherry trees!"

This was another meal that nobody ever forgot. Even the two hired men sitting under another tree devouring the delicious pudding, paused to hear Benny laugh. Nowadays those two men sometimes meet Henry—but that's another story. Anyway, they never will forget that cherry slump made by Irish Mary.

Almost as soon as lunch was over Benny rolled over on the grass and went to sleep, his head, as usual, on the dog's back. But the others worked on steadily. Mrs. McAllister kept an eye on them from the screened porch without their knowledge.

"Just see how those children keep at it," she said to her son. "There is good stuff in them. I would like to know where they come from."

Dr. McAllister said nothing. He sauntered out into the orchard when he thought they had worked long enough. He paid them four dollars and gave them all the cherries they could carry, although they tried to object.

"You see, you're better than most pickers, because you're so cheerful."

He noticed that they did not all leave the yard at the same time.

When the cherry pickers returned to their little home they examined everything carefully. Nothing had been disturbed. The door was still shut, and the milk and butter stood untouched in the refrigerator. They made a hilarious meal of raw cherries and bread and butter, and before the stars came out they were fast asleep—happy and dreamless.

That evening, very much later, a young man sat in his study with the evening paper. He read the news idly, and was just on the point of tossing the paper aside when this advertisement caught his eye:

Lost. Four children, aged thirteen, twelve, ten and five. Somewhere around the region of Middlesex and Townsend. $5000 reward for information.

James Henry Cordyce

"Whew!" whistled the young man. "James Henry Cordyce!"

He sat in perfect silence for a long time, thinking. Then he went to bed. But long after he had gone upstairs he whistled again, and could have been heard to say-if anyone had been awake to hear it—"James Henry Cordyce! Of all people!"

THE RACE

The Cordyce Steel Mills stood a little aside from the city of Greenfield, as if they were a little too good to associate with common factories. James Henry Cordyce sat in a huge leather chair in his private office. He was a man nearly sixty years of age whose dark brown hair was still untouched by gray. He had rather hard lines around his mouth, but softer ones around his eyes. Printed on the ground-glass top of his door were these words in black and gold:

J. H. Cordyce—President

Private

Once a year J. H. Cordyce allowed himself a holiday. If he had a weakness, it was for healthy boys—boys running without their hats, boys jumping, boys throwing rings, boys swimming, boys vaulting with a long pole. And in company with three other extremely rich men he arranged, once a year, a Field Day for the town of Intervale. The men attended it in person, and supplied all the money. This was Field Day.

All through the spring and early summer months, boys were in training for miles around, getting ready for Intervale's Field Day. And not only boys, but men also, old and young, and girls of all ages into the bargain. Prizes were offered for tennis, baseball, rowing, swimming, running, and every imaginable type of athletic feat. But usually the interest of the day centered on a free-for-all race of one mile, which everyone enjoyed, and a great many people entered. A prize of twenty-five dollars was offered to the winner of this race, and also a silver trophy cup with little wings on its handles. Sometimes this cup was won by a middle-aged man, sometimes by a girl, and sometimes by a trained athlete. Mr. Cordyce smiled in his eyes as he closed his desk, ordered his limousine, and went out and locked the door of his office. The mill had been closed down for the day. Everyone attended Field Day.

Henry was washing the concrete drives at Dr. McAllister's at this moment. He heard the doctor call to him from the road, so he promptly turned off the hose and ran out to see what was wanted.

"Hop in," commanded the doctor, not stopping his engine. "You ought to go to see the stunts at the athletic meet. It's Field Day."

Henry did not wish to delay the doctor, so he "hopped in."

"Can't go myself," said Dr. McAllister. "I'll just drop you on the ground. There's no charge for admittance. You just watch all the events and report to me who wins."

Henry tried to explain to his friend that he ought to be working, but there was actually no time. And when he found himself seated on the bleachers and the stunts began, he forgot everything in the world except the exciting events before his eyes.

Henry had no pencil, but he had an excellent memory. He repeated over and over, the name of each winner as it appeared on the huge signboard.

It was nearly eleven o'clock when the free-for-all running race was announced.

"What do they mean—free-for-all?" asked Henry of a small boy at his side.

"Why, just anybody," explained the boy, curiously. "Didn't you ever see one? Didn't you see the one last year?"

"No," said Henry.

The boy laughed. "That was a funny one," he said. "There was a college runner in it, and a couple of fat men, and some girls—lots of people. And the little colored boy over there won it. You just ought to have seen that boy run! He went so fast you couldn't see his legs.

Beat the college runner, you know."

Henry gazed at the winner of last year's race. He was smaller than Henry, but apparently older. In a few minutes Henry had quietly left his place on the bleachers. When the boy turned to speak to him again, he was gone.

He had gone, in fact, to the dressing room, where boys of all sizes were putting on sandals and running trunks.

A man stepped up to him quickly.

"Want to enter?" he asked. "No time to waste."

"Yes," replied Henry.

The man tossed him a pair of white shoes and some blue trunks. He liked the look of Henry's face as he paused to ask in an undertone, "Where did you train?"

"Never trained," replied Henry.

"I suppose you know these fellows have been training all year?" observed the man. "You don't expect to win?"

"Oh, no!" replied Henry, apparently shocked at the idea. "But it's lots of fun to run, you know." He was dressed and ready by this time. How light he felt! He felt as if he could almost fly. Presently the contestants were all marshalled out to the running track. Henry was Number 4.

Now, Henry had never been trained to run, but the boy possessed an unusual quantity of common sense. "It's a mile race," he thought to himself, "and it's the second half mile that counts." So it happened that this was the main thought in his mind when the starter's gong sounded and the racers shot away down the track. In almost no time, Henry was far behind the first half of the runners. But strangely enough, he did not seem to mind this greatly.

"It's fun to run, anyhow," he thought.

It was fun, certainly. He felt as if his limbs were strung together on springs. He ran easily, without effort, each step bounding into the next like an elastic.

After a few minutes of this, Henry had a new thought.

"Now you've tried how easy you can run, let's see how fast you can run!"

And then not only Henry himself, but the enormous crowd as well, began to see how fast he could run. Slowly he gained on the fellow ahead of him, and passed him. With the next fellow as a goal, he gradually crept alongside, and passed him with a spurt. The crowd shouted itself hoarse. The field all along the course was black with people. Henry could hear them cheering for Number 4, as he pounded by. Six runners remained ahead of him. Here was the kind of race the crowd loved; not an easily won affair between two runners, but a gradual victory between the best runner and overpowering odds. Henry could see the finish-flag now in the distance. He began to spurt. He passed Numbers 14 and 3. He passed 25, 6, and 1 almost in a bunch. Number 16 remained ahead. Then Henry began to think of winning. How much the twenty-five dollar prize would mean to Jess and the rest! Number 16 must be passed.

"I'm going to win this race!" he said quietly in his own mind. "I'll bet you I am!" The thought lent him speed.

"Number 4! Number 4!" yelled the crowd. Henry did not know that the fellow ahead had been ahead all the way, and just because he —Henry—had slowly gained over them all, the crowd loved him best.

Henry waited until he could have touched him. He was within three yards of the wire. He bent double, and put all his energy into the last elastic bound. He passed Number 16, and shot under the wire.

Then the crowd went wild. It scrambled over and under the fence, cheering and blowing its horns. Henry felt himself lifted on many shoulders and carried panting up to the reviewing stand. He bowed laughing at the sea of faces, and took the silver cup with its little wings in a sort of dream. It is a wonder he did not lose the envelope containing the prize, for he hardly realized when he took it what it was.

Then someone said, "What's your name, boy?"

Henry felt himself lifted on many shoulders

That called him to earth. He had to think quickly under cover of getting his breath.

"Henry James," he replied. This was perfectly true, as far as it went. In a moment the enormous signboard flashed out the name:

HENRY JAMES No. 4. AGE 13

WINNER OF FREE-FOR-ALL

Meanwhile the man of the dressing room was busy locating Mr. Cordyce of the Cordyce Mills. He knew that was exactly the kind of story that old James Henry would like.

"Yes, sir," he said smiling. "I said to him, 'You don't expect to win, of course.' And he says to me, 'Oh, no, but it's lots of fun to run, you know.'"

"Thank you, sir," returned Mr. Cordyce. "That's a good story. Bring the youngster over here, if you don't mind."

When Henry appeared, a trifle shaken out of his daze and anxious only to get away, Mr. Cordyce stretched out his hand. "I like your spirit, my boy," he said. "I like your running, too. But it's your spirit that I like best. Don't ever lose it."

"Thank you," said Henry, shaking hands. And there was only one in the whole crowd that knew who was shaking hands with whom, least of all James Henry and Henry James.

MORE EDUCATION

With twenty-five dollars in his hand, Henry felt like a millionaire as he edged through the crowd to the gate.

"That's the boy," he heard many people say when he was forced to hold his silver cup in view out of harm's way.

When Dr. McAllister drove into his yard he found a boy washing the concrete drives as calmly as if nothing had happened. He chuckled quietly, for he had stopped at the FairGrounds for a few minutes himself, and held a little conversation with the scorekeeper. When Henry faithfully repeated the list of winners, however, he said nothing about it.

"What are you going to do with the prize?" queried Dr. McAllister.

"Put it in the savings bank, I guess," replied Henry.

"Do you have an account?" asked his friend.

"No, but Jess says it's high time we started one."

"Good for Jess," said the doctor absently. "I remember an old uncle of mine who put two hundred dollars in the savings bank and forgot all about it. He left it there till he died, and it came to me. It amounted to sixteen hundred dollars."

"Whew!" said Henry.

"He left it alone for over forty years, you see," explained Dr. McAllister.

When Henry arrived at his little home in the woods with the twenty-five dollars (for he never thought of putting it in the bank before Jess saw it), he found a delicious lunch waiting for him. Jess had boiled the little vegetables in clear water, and the moment they were done she had drained off the water in a remarkable drainer, and healed them on the biggest dish with melted butter on top.

His family almost forgot to eat while Henry recounted the details of the exciting race. And when he showed them the silver cup and the money they actually did stop eating, hungry as they were.

"I said my name was Henry James," repeated Henry.

"That's all right. So it is," affirmed Jess. "It's clever, too. You can use that name for your bank book."

"So I can!" said Henry, delighted. "I'll put it in the bank this very afternoon. And by the way, I brought something for dinner tonight."

Jess looked in the bag. There were a dozen smooth, brown potatoes.

"I know how to cook those," said Jess, nodding her head wisely. "You just wait!"

"Can't wait, hardly," Henry called back as he went to work.

When he had gone, Benny frolicked around noisily with the dog.

"Benny," Jess exclaimed suddenly, as she hung her dish towels up to dry, "it's high time you learned to read."

"No school now," said Benny hopefully.

"No, but I can teach you. If I only had a primer!"

"Let's make one," suggested Violet, shaking her hair back. "We have saved all the wrapping paper off the bundles, you know."

Jess was staring off into space, as she always did when she had a bright idea.

"Violet," she cried at last, "remember those chips? We could whittle out letters like type—make each letter backwards, you know."

"And stamp them on paper!" finished Violet.

"There would be only twenty-six in all. It wouldn't be awfully hard," said Jess. "We wouldn't bother with capitals."

"What could we use for ink?" Violet wondered, wrinkling her forehead.

"Blackberry juice!" cried Jess. The two girls clapped their hands. "Won't Henry be surprised when he finds that Benny can read?"

Now from this conversation Benny gathered that this type-business would take his sisters quite a while to prepare. So he was not much worried about his part of the work. In fact, he sorted out chips very cheerfully and watched his teachers with interest as they dug carefully around the letters with the two knives.

"We'll teach him two words to begin with," said Jess. "Then we won't have to make the whole alphabet at once. Let's begin to teach him."

"That's easy," agreed Violet. "And then we won't have to make but two letters, s and e."

"And the other word will be me," cried Jess. "So only three pieces of type in all, Violet."

Jess cut the wiggly s, because she had the better knife, while Violet struggled with the e. Then Jess cut a wonderful m while Violet sewed the primer down the back, and gathered a cupful of blackberries. As she sat by, crushing the juice from the berries with a stick, Jess planned the ink pad.

"We'll have to use a small piece of the wash-cloth, I'm afraid," she said at last.

But finally they were obliged to cut off only the uneven bits of cloth which hung around the edges. These they used for stuffing for the pad, and covered them with a pocket which Violet carefully ripped from her apron. When this was sewed firmly into place, and put into a small saucer, Jess poured on the purple juice.

Even Benny came up on his hands and knees to watch her stamp the first s. It came out beautifully on the first page of the primer, purple and clean-cut. The e was almost as good, and as for the m, Jess' hand shook with pure pride as she stamped it evenly on the page. At last the two words were completed. In fact, they were done long before Benny had the slightest idea his sisters were ready for him.

He came willingly enough for his first lesson, but he could not tell the two words apart.

"Don't you see, Benny?" Jess explained patiently. "This one with the wiggly s says see?" But Benny did not "see."

"I'll tell you, Jess," said Violet at last. "Let's print each word again on a separate card. That's the way they do it at school. And then let him point to see."

The girls did this, using squares of stiff brown paper. Then they called Benny. Very carefully, Jess explained again which word said see, hissing like a huge snake to show him how the s sounded. Then she mixed the cards and said encouragingly, "Now, Benny, point to s-s-s-ee."

Benny did not move. He sat with his finger on his lip.

But the children were nearly petrified with astonishment to see Watch cock his head on one side and gravely put his paw on the center of the word! Now, this was only an accident. Watch did not really know one of the words from the other. But Benny thought he did. And was he going to let a dog get ahead of him? Not Benny! In less time than it takes to tell it, Benny had learned both words perfectly.

"Good old Watch," said Jess.

"It isn't really hard at all," said Benny. "Is it, Watch?"

During all this experiment Jess had not forgotten her dinner. When you are living outdoors all the time you do not forget things like that. In fact both girls had learned to tell the time very accurately by the sun.

Jess started up a beautiful little fire of cones. As they turned into red-hot ashes and began to topple over one by one into the glowing pile, Jess laughed delightedly. She had already scrubbed the smooth potatoes and dried them carefully. She now poked them one by one into the glowing ashes with a stick from a birch tree. Whenever a potato lit up dangerously she gave it a poke into a new position. And when Henry found her, she was just rolling the charred balls out onto the flat stones.

"Burned 'em up?" queried Henry.

"Burned, nothing!" cried Jess energetically. "You just wait!"

"Can't wait, hardly," replied Henry, smiling.

"You said that a long time ago," said Benny.

"Well, isn't it true?" demanded Henry, rolling his brother over on the pine needles.

"Come," said Violet breathlessly, forgetting to ring the bell.

"Hold them with leaves," directed Jess, "because they're terribly hot. Knock them on the side and scoop them out with a spoon and put butter on top."

The children did as the little cook requested, sprinkled on a little salt from the salt shaker, and took a taste.

"Ah!" said Henry.

"It's good," said Benny blissfully. It was about the most successful meal of all, in fact. When the children in later years recalled their different feasts, they always came back to the baked potatoes roasted in the ashes of the pine cones. Henry said it was because they were poked with a black-birch stick. Benny said it was because Jess nearly burned them up. Jess herself said maybe it was the remarkable salt shaker which had to stand on its head always, because there was no floor to it.

After supper the children still were not too sleepy to show Henry the new primer, and allow Benny to display his first reading lesson. Henry, greatly taken with the idea, sat up until it was almost dark, chipping out the remaining letters of the alphabet.

If you should ever care to see this interesting primer, which was finally ten pages in length, you might examine this faithful copy of its first page, which required four days for its completion:

```
                                        page 1
    See
    me
    See   me
    O  O  see  me
    Come
    Come  to  me
    Come  to  see  me
    cat 🐱
    rat 〜
```

Henry always insisted that the rat's tail was too long, but Jess said his knife must have slipped when he was making the a, so they were even, after all.

GINSENG

What Dr. McAllister ever did before Henry began to work for him would be hard to guess.

There were certainly as many duties always waiting for him as he had time to do. And it made no difference to the industrious boy what the job was. Nothing was too hard or too dirty for him to attempt.

One day the doctor set him the task of clearing out his little laboratory. The boy washed bottles, pasted labels, and cleaned instruments for one whole morning. And more than one broken flask on its way to the rubbish heap was carefully carried up the hill to the hidden family.

While Henry was busy carefully lettering a sticky label, he noticed a young man in the outer office who was talking with the doctor.

"Can you tell me if this is real ginseng?" Henry heard him say.

"It certainly is," returned Dr. McAllister. "They will give you two dollars a pound for the root at any of the drug stores."

Henry ventured to steal a peep, and found he could readily see the plant the man was holding. It was about a foot high with branching leaves and a fine feathery white flower. Henry knew it was exactly the same white puffball that he had noticed in Violet's vase that very morning.

When the young man had gone, Henry said, "I know where I can find a whole lot of that plant."

"Is that so?" replied the doctor kindly. "It's only the root, you know, that is valuable. But any one who wants the bother of digging it up can sell any quantity of it."

When Henry went home at noon he related enough of this incident to set his sisters to work in good earnest. They started out with both knives and two strong iron spoons, and the kettle. And with Benny to run about finding every white flower he could, the girls succeeded, with a great deal of hard digging, in finding enormous quantities of ginseng root. In fact, that first afternoon's work resulted in a kettle full, not counting a single leaf or stem. Henry was delighted when he saw the result of their work, and took it the next day to the largest drug store, where he received three dollars for the roots.

Without any hesitation Henry paid a visit to the dry-goods store, and came home with a pair of new brown stockings for Benny. That was a great day in the woods. Benny gave them no peace at all until they had admired his wonderful new stockings, and felt of each rib.

There had been one other thing that Benny had given them no peace about. On the night when the children had crept so quietly away from the baker's wife, Jess had forgotten to take Benny's bear. This bear was a poor looking creature, which had once been an expensive bright-eyed Teddy-bear made of brown plush. But Benny had taken it to bed every single night for three years, and had loved it day by day, so that it was not attractive to anyone but himself. Both eyes were gone, and its body was very limp, but Benny had certainly suffered a great deal trying to sleep in a strange bed without his beloved bear.

Jess, therefore, had plans on foot, the moment she saw Benny's new stockings. She washed the old brown stockings with their many neat darns, and hung them up to dry. And early in the afternoon she and Violet sat with the workbag between them, each with a stocking.

With Benny sitting by to watch proceedings, Jess mapped out a remarkable Teddy-bear. One stocking, carefully trimmed, made the head and body, while the other furnished material for two arms, two legs, and the stuffing. Jess worked hard over the head, pushing the padding well into the blunt nose. Violet embroidered two beautiful eyes in black and white, and a jet black nose-tip.

"You must make a tail, too, Jessy," said Benny, watching her snip the brown rags.

"Bears don't have tails, Benny," argued Jess—although she wasn't exactly sure she was right. "Your old bear didn't have any tail, you know."

"But this bear has a tail, though," returned Benny, knowing that Jess would put on two tails if he insisted.

And it was true. His bear finally did have a tail.

"What kind of tail?" asked Jess helplessly at last. "Bushy, long and slim, or cotton-tail?"

"Long and slim," decided Benny with great satisfaction, "so I can pull it."

"Benny!" cried Jess, laughing in spite of herself. But she made a tail, long and slim, exactly as Benny ordered, and sewed it on very tightly, so that it might be "pulled" if desired. She fastened on the legs and arms with flat hinges, so the bear might sit down easily, and added at last a pair of cunning flappy ears and a gay collar of braided red string from a bundle.

"What's his name, Jessy?" inquired Benny, when the wonderful bear was finally handed over to him.

"His name?" repeated Jess. "Well, you know he's a new bear; he isn't your old one, so I wouldn't call him Teddy."

"Oh, no," said Benny, shocked. "This is not Teddy. This has a pretty tail."

"Of course," agreed Jess, trying not to laugh. "Well, you know we sold that ginseng to pay for your new stockings. And if you hadn't had your new ones, we couldn't have made this bear out of your old ones."

"You want his name to be Stockings?" asked Benny politely.

"Stockings? No," answered Jess. "I was thinking of 'Ginseng.'"

"Ginseng?" echoed Benny, thinking deeply. "That's a nice name. All right, I think Ginseng will be a good bear, if Watchie doesn't bark at him." And from that moment the bear's name was Ginseng as long as he lived, and he lived to be a very old bear indeed.

TROUBLE

The days went merrily by for the freight-car family. Hardly a day passed, however, without some exciting adventure. Mrs. McAllister, finding out in some way that Violet was a clever seamstress, sent home fine linen handkerchiefs for her to them. Each one had a tiny colored rose in the corner, and Violet was delighted with the dainty work. She sat sewing daily by the swimming pool while Benny sailed wonderful boats of chips, and waded around to his heart's content.

The freight-car pantry now held marvelous dishes rescued from the dump; such rarities as a regular bread knife, a blue and gold soap dish, and half of a real cut-glass bowl.

Henry proudly deposited thirty-one dollars in the savings bank under the name of Henry James, and worked eagerly for his kind friend, who never asked him any more embarrassing questions.

Benny actually learned to read fairly well. The girls occupied their time making balsam pillows for the four beds, and trying to devise wonderful meals out of very little material. Violet kept a different bouquet daily in the little vase. She had a perfect genius for arranging three purple irises to look like a picture, or a single wood lily with its leaves like a Japanese print. Each day the children enjoyed a cooked dinner, filling in the chinks with perfect satisfaction with bread and butter, or bread and milk, or bread and cheese. They named their queer house, "Home for Tramps," and printed this title in fancy lettering inside the car.

One day Jess began to teach Benny a little arithmetic. He learned very readily that two and one make three.

"I knew that before," he said cheerfully. But it was a different matter when Jess proposed to him that two minus one left one.

"No, it does not leave one," said Benny indignantly. "It left two."

"Why, Benny!" cried Jess in astonishment. "Suppose you had two apples and I took away one, wouldn't you have one left?"

"You never would," objected Benny with confidence.

"No, but supposing Watch took one," suggested Jess.

One day the stranger was allowed to see Violet

"Watchie wouldn't take one, either," said Benny. "Would you, doggie?"

Watch opened one eye and wagged his tail. Jess looked at Violet in despair. "What shall I do with him?" she asked.

Violet took out her chalk and printed clearly on the outside of the freight car the following example:

$$2 - 1 =$$

"Now, Benny, don't you see," she began, "that if you have two things, and somebody takes away one, that you must have one left?"

"I'll show you myself," agreed Benny finally with resignation. "Now see the 2?" He actually made a respectable figure 2 on the freight car. "Now, here's a nice 1. Now, s'pose I take away the 1, don't you see the 2's left right on the car?" He covered the figure 1 with his chubby hand and looked about at his audience expectantly.

Jess rolled over against a tree trunk and laughed till she nearly cried. Violet laughed until she really did cry. And here we come to the first unpleasant incident in the story of the runaway children.

Violet could not stop crying, apparently, and Jess soon made up her mind that she was really ill. She helped her carefully into the car, and heaped all the pine needles around and under her, making her the softest bed she could. Then she wet clothes in the cool water of the brook and laid them across her little sister's hot forehead.

"How glad I am that it is time for Henry to come!" she said to herself, holding Violet's slender brown hands in her cool ones.

Henry came promptly at the usual time. He thought she had a cold, he said. And this seemed likely, for Violet began to cough gently while the rest ate a hasty supper.

"We don't want to let her go to a hospital if we can possibly help it," said Henry, more troubled than he cared to show. "If she goes there we'll have to give her name, and then Grandfather will find us surely."

Jess agreed, and together the two older children kept changing the cool clothes on Violet's aching head. But about ten o'clock that night Violet had a chill. She shivered and shook, and her teeth chattered so that Jess could plainly hear them. Apparently nothing could warm the little girl, although she was completely packed in hay and pine needles.

"I'm going down to Dr. McAllister's," said Henry quietly. "I'm afraid Violet is very ill."

Nobody ever knew how fast he ran down the hill. Even in his famous race, Henry hardly touched his present speed. He was so thoroughly frightened that he never stopped to notice how quickly the doctor seemed to understand what was wanted. He did not even notice that he did not have to tell the doctor which way to drive his car in order to reach the hill. When the car reached the road at the base of the hill, Dr. McAllister said shortly, "Stay here in the car," and disappeared up the hill alone.

When the doctor returned he was carrying Violet in his arms. Jess and Benny and Watch were following closely. Nobody spoke during the drive to the McAllister house as they flew through the darkness. When they stopped at last, the doctor said three words to his mother, who opened the door anxiously.

The three words were, "Pneumonia, I'm afraid." They all heard it.

Irish Mary appeared from the kitchen with hot-water bottles and warm blankets, and Mrs. McAllister flew around, opening beds and bringing pillows. A trained nurse in a white dress appeared like magic from nowhere in particular. They all worked as best they could to get the sick child warmed up. Soon the hot blankets, hot water, and steaming drinks began to take effect and the shivering stopped.

Mrs. McAllister left the sick room then, to attend to the other children. Henry and Benny were left in a large spare room with a double bed. Jess was put in a little dressing room just out of Mrs. McAllister's own room. Upon receiving assurances that Violet was warm again, they went to sleep.

But Violet was not out of danger, for she soon grew as hot as she had been cold. And the doctor never left her side until ten o'clock the next morning. Violet, although very ill, did not have pneumonia.

At about nine o'clock the doctor had a visitor. It was a man who said he would wait. He waited in the cool front parlor for over half an hour. Then Benny drifted in.

"Where is the doctor?" asked the man sharply of Benny.

"He's upstairs," answered Benny readily.

"This means a lot of money to him, if he only knew it," said the visitor impatiently.

"Oh, that wouldn't make any difference," Benny replied with great assurance as he started to go out again. But the man caught him.

"What do you mean by that, sonny?" he asked curiously. "What's he doing?"

"He's taking care of my sister Violet. She's sick."

"And you mean he wouldn't leave her even if I gave him a lot of money?"

"Yes, that's it," said Benny politely. "That's what I mean."

The visitor seemed to restrain his impatience with a great effort. "You see, I've lost a little boy somewhere," he said. "The doctor knows where he is, I think. He would be about as old as you are."

"Well, if you don't find him, you can have me, I shouldn't wonder," observed Benny comfortingly. "I like you."

"You do?" said the man in surprise.

"That's because you've got such a nice, soft suit on," explained Benny, stroking the man's knee gently. The gentleman laughed heartily.

"No, I guess it's because you have such a nice, soft laugh," said Benny, changing his mind. The fact was that Benny himself did not know why he liked this stranger who was so gruff at times and so pleasant at others. He finally accepted the man's invitation and climbed into his lap to see his dog's picture in his watch, feeling of the "nice soft suit," on the way. The doctor found him here when he came down at ten o'clock.

"Better go and find Watch, Benny," suggested the doctor.

"Perhaps some day I'll come again," observed Benny to his new friend. "I like your dog, and I'm sorry he's dead." With that he scampered off to find Watch, who was very much alive.

"I expected you, Mr. Cordyce," said the doctor smiling, "only not quite so soon."

"I came the moment I heard your name hinted at," said James Cordyce. "My chauffeur heard two workmen say that you knew where my four grandchildren were. That's all I waited to hear. Is it true? And where are they?"

"That was one of them," said the doctor quietly.

"That was one of them!" repeated the man. "That beautiful little boy?"

"Yes, he is beautiful," assented Dr. McAllister. "They all are. The only trouble is, they're all frightened to death to think of you finding them."

"How do you know that?" said Mr. Cordyce, sharply.

"They've changed their name. At least the older boy did. In public, too."

"What did he change it to?"

Dr. McAllister watched his visitor's face closely while he pronounced the name clearly, "Henry James."

A flood of recollections passed over the man's face, and he flushed deeply.

"That boy!" he exclaimed. "That wonderful running boy?"

Then events began to move along rapidly.

CAUGHT

"They never will go with you in this world," declared Mrs. McAllister finally to the distracted grandfather, "unless you give us time to break the news gradually. And above all, when Violet is so ill."

"Couldn't I see them?" begged the man, almost like a boy. "I could pretend I was a friend of yours, visiting you, who liked children. I would promise not to tell them until you consented."

"That might do," said Dr. McAllister. "If they grew to like you before they knew who you were, it would make things easier, certainly."

So James Henry Cordyce's chauffeur was sent for a gold-monogrammed suitcase and his young man to wait upon him, and Irish Mary held up her hands in despair when she learned for whom she must cook.

"Don't you worry, Mary Bridget Flynn," said Dr. McAllister with emphasis. "You could cook for the King of England! Just make one of your peach shortcakes for lunch and broil a chicken, and I'll answer for him."

When lunch time came J. H. Cordyce saw all his grandchildren except Violet. He smiled with delight when he saw Jess coming down the stairs in her womanly fashion. Henry shook hands with him before he sat down, but he kept glancing at the stranger all through the meal.

"Where have I seen that man before?" he thought.

Mrs. McAllister had given the children's names clearly when she introduced them—Jess, Benny, and Henry. Henry James, she had added. But she had not added the man's name.

"She forgot," thought Jess. "Because she knows him so well, she thinks we do."

But although nameless, the stranger caught their attention. He told them wonderful stories about a steel rail which held up an entire bridge until the people had time to get off, about his collie dog, about a cucumber in his garden, growing inside of a glass bottle. Henry was interested. Benny was fascinated.

"I'd like to see the cucumber," said Benny, pausing in the middle of his shortcake.

"Would you, indeed?" said Mr. Cordyce, delighted. "Some day, if Mrs. McAllister is willing, you and I will ride over to my garden and pick it."

"And we'll bring it to Violet?" asked Benny, waiting breathlessly for an answer.

"We'll bring it to Violet," agreed Mr. Cordyce, resuming his shortcake.

After lunch he went to sleep in the easy-chair in the doctor's big office. That is, he threw his head back and shut his eyes, and breathed very heavily. Jess went through the room once with ice water, humming, for Violet was better. But the moment she saw the stranger asleep, she stopped her singing abruptly and tiptoed the rest of the way. Then suddenly she turned around and came back, and very carefully shoved a cushion under the man's feet. It was so gently done that even if he had been really asleep, he would never have woken up. As it was, he could not resist opening one eye the slightest crack to see the bright chestnut hair as it passed out of sight.

"No," he thought to himself, "if she really hated me, she would never have done that."

But the children were very far from hating him. They liked him immensely. And when at last, one day, he was allowed to see Violet, and came softly into her room with a nosegay of fragrant English double violets, for her, they loved him. He won all their hearts when he patted her dark head and told her very simply that he was sorry she had been sick.

It would be hard to say that J. H. Cordyce ever had a favorite grandchild, but certainly his manner with Violet was very gentle. It was clear to everyone, even to the anxious nurse, that the stranger was not tiring the sick child. He told her in a pleasant everyday voice about his garden and his greenhouses where the violets came from—about the old Swede gardener who always said he must "vater the wi-lets."

"I'd love to see him," said Violet earnestly.

"How long are you going to stay here?" Benny piped up.

It was not altogether a polite question, but it was clear to them all that Benny wanted him to stay, so they all laughed.

"As long as they'll let me, my boy," answered the stranger quietly. Then he left the sick room, for he knew he should not stay long.

But something in the man's last sentence rang in Henry's ears. He repeated it over and over in his mind, trying to remember where he had heard that same voice say "my boy." He made an excuse to work in the flower beds along the veranda, in order to glance occasionally at the man's face, as he sat under a tree reading.

Often Henry thought he had caught hold of his truant memory. Then the man turned his head and he lost it again altogether. But suddenly it came to him, as the man smiled over his book—it was the man who had shaken hands with him on the day of the race! And he had said, "I like your spirit, my boy." That was it.

Henry sat down out of sight and weeded geraniums for a few moments. It is a wonder he did not pull up geraniums instead of weeds, his mind was so far away.

"I didn't remember him at first, because I was so jolly excited when he shook hands with me," decided Henry. Then he was apparently thunderstruck afresh. He sat with his weeder on his knee and his mouth open. "He's the man who passed me the cup with the wings!" He stole another look around the corner, and this satisfied him. "Same man exactly," he said.

When he had finished the flower bed he thought he heard the young doctor moving in the office. He stuck his head in the open door. The doctor sat at his desk, taking notes from a book.

"Do you know who presented the prizes for Field Day?" asked Henry curiously. "Know what his name was?"

"James Cordyce, of the Steel Mills," replied the doctor carelessly. "J. H. Cordyce—over in Greenfield."

Dr. McAllister, to all appearances, returned to his notes. His eyes were lowered, at any rate. But for Henry the skies were reeling. He withdrew his head and sat still on the step. That delightful man, his grandfather? It was impossible. He was too young, to begin with. Henry expected a white-haired gentleman with a cane and a terrible voice. But all the time, he knew in his soul that it was not only possible, but really true. He recalled the man's reply to Benny's direct question—he had said he was going to stay as long as they would let him. Could it be that the man knew them without introducing himself? A perfect torrent of thoughts assailed Henry as he sat crouched on the office steps. It was clear to him now that Mrs. McAllister had failed to mention his name on purpose. It was a wonder Benny hadn't asked what it was, long before this. He noticed that the man was getting out of his chair under the trees.

"It's now or never," thought Henry. "I've got to know!"

He walked eagerly after the man who was going toward the garden with his back turned. Henry easily caught up with him, breathing with difficulty. The man turned around.

"Are you James Henry Cordyce of Greenfield?" painted Henry.

"I am, my boy," returned the man with a long look. "Does that question of yours mean that you know that I know that you are Henry

James Cordyce?"

"Yes," said Henry, simply.

The man's eyes filled with tears, and J. H. Cordyce of the Steel Mills shook hands for the third time with his grandson, H. J. Cordyce of the Home for Tramps.

A NEW GRANDFATHER

In less than an hour the town was buzzing with the news. The chauffeur told the maids and the maids told the grocery man, and the grocery man went from house to house telling that old James Cordyce had found his four grandchildren at last. In fact the biggest part of the town knew it before the children themselves.

Jess and Benny came across the lawn to select some white moonflowers for Violet's tray. They were just in time to hear Henry say, "But, Grandfather—"

"Grandfather!" echoed Jess, whirling around to gaze at them.

"Yes, Jess," said Henry eagerly. "He's the man we've been running away from all this time."

"I thought you were old," observed Benny. "And awf'ly cross. Jess said so."

"I didn't know, Benny," said Jess turning pink. To think of running away from this kind friend!

But her grandfather did not seem to mind. He stroked her short silky hair and proposed that they all go up into Violet's room with the moonflowers. There was no stopping Benny. He rushed into Violet's room, dragging his grandfather by one hand, and shouting, "It's Grandfather, Violet, and he's nice, after all, I shouldn't wonder!"

When Violet at last understood just what Benny was trying to tell, she was perfectly happy to rest against her ruffled pillows with one hand curled about her grandfather's arm, and listen to the rest.

"Where have you been living?" demanded Mr. Cordyce at last.

The whole company looked at each other, even Dr. McAllister and his mother. Then they all laughed as if they never would stop.

"You just ought to see!" observed Dr. McAllister, wiping his eyes.

"What?" said the children all at once. "You never saw it in the daytime!"

"You don't mean it!" returned the doctor, teasing them. "I have seen it quite a number of times in the daytime."

"Seen what, in heaven's name?" asked Mr. Cordyce at last.

Then they told him, interrupting each other to tell about the beds of pine needles, the wonderful dishes, the freight-car roof over all, the fireplace, and the swimming pool.

"That's where Violet got her bronchitis," observed the doctor, "sitting by that pool. She shouldn't have done it. I thought so from the first."

"You thought so?" repeated Henry, puzzled. "How did you know she sat by it? I'm sure I didn't myself."

"I was your most frequent visitor," declared the doctor, enjoying himself hugely.

"I hope you were our only one," said Jess with her mouth open.

"Well, I think I was," said the doctor. "The first night after Henry mowed my lawn I followed him as far as the hill to see where he lived."

"Why did you do that?" interrupted Mr. Cordyce.

"I liked his looks," returned the doctor. "And I noticed that he didn't tell much about himself, so I was curious."

"But you surely didn't see the freight car then," said Jess.

"No, but I came back that night and hunted around," replied Dr. McAllister.

"At about eleven o'clock!" Henry cried. The doctor assented.

"Our rabbit!" said Henry and Jess together.

"I made as little noise as possible when I saw the freight car. Then I saw the door move, so I thought someone was inside. And when I heard the dog bark I was sure of it, and went home."

"But you came back?" questioned Jess.

"Yes, every time I knew all of you were safe in my garden, I made you a little visit, just to be sure you were having enough to eat, and enough dishes." The doctor laughed. "When I found you had a strainer, and a vase of flowers, and a salt-shaker, and a cut-glass punch bowl, I stopped worrying."

"Didn't you suspect they were my children?" demanded Mr. Cordyce. "Didn't you see my advertisement? Why didn't you notify me at once?"

"They were having such a good time," confessed the doctor. "And I was, too. I just wanted to see how long they could manage their own affairs. It was all tremendously interesting. Why, that boy and girl of yours are born business managers, Mr. Cordyce!"

Mr. Cordyce took note of this.

"But I don't see, yet, how you knew Violet sat by the pool," said Jess curiously.

"You couldn't know that, of course," replied the doctor. "I went up twice when I knew Henry had taken the dog down to my barn to catch rats. I hid behind a big white rock with a flat top."

"That's Lookout Rock," explained Jess, "where we used to let Benny watch for Henry. But we didn't hear you."

"No," said Dr. McAllister. "I didn't even snap a twig those times. But I had the very best time when I went with Mother."

"Have you seen it, too?" cried the children.

"I have, indeed!" returned Mrs. McAllister. "I have even had a drink from your well."

"Everyone has seen it but me," said Mr. Cordyce patiently.

"We'll show it to you!" screamed Benny. "And I'll show you my wheels made on a cart, and my bed out of hay, and my pink cup!"

"Good for you, Benny," said Mr. Cordyce, pleased. "When Violet gets well, we'll all go up there, and if you'll show me your house, I'll show you mine."

"Have you got a house?" asked Benny in surprise.

"Yes. You can live there with me, if you like," replied Mr. Cordyce. "I have been looking for you for nearly two months."

Under Mrs. McAllister's wonderful care, Violet soon became strong again. But she had been skipping around the garden for several days before the doctor would allow the visit to the freight-car house. When at last the whole party started out in the great limousine, many people looked out of their windows to watch after Mr. Cordyce and his grandchildren. Many of them knew Henry as the boy who won the race, and were glad that he had found such a friend.

But when the children reached their beloved home they were like wild things. Watch capered about furiously, taking little swims in the pool and sniffing at all the dear old familiar things. Mr. Cordyce seated himself on a rock and watched them all, exchanging a glance now and then with Mrs. McAllister and her son.

"See our building," shouted Benny, for that was what he always called the fireplace. "It burns really, too. And this is the well, and this is the dishpan, and this is the 'refrigerator'!"

At last every one climbed into the car itself, and Mr. Cordyce saw the beds, the cash account on the wall, the wonderful shelf, and each separate dish. Each dish had a story of its own.

"That's more than my dishes have," observed Mr. Cordyce.

Mrs. McAllister, who knew what his dishes were, was silent.

They ate chicken sandwiches on the very same tablecloth, and Benny drank from his pink cup, and Watch couldn't understand why they went away at all.

But it was a trifle cool on the hill now when the sun began to sink, and after rolling the door shut, they left regretfully.

"Tomorrow," suggested Mr. Cordyce, as they drove home, "will you all come and see my house?"

"Oh, yes," agreed the children happily, little dreaming what was in store for them on the next day and all the days to come.

A UNITED FAMILY

Mr. Cordyce had been planning this day for more than a week. He had sent his most trusted foreman to his own beautiful home, to superintend matters there. The house was being remodeled entirely, after Mr. Cordyce's own plans, and everywhere were carpenters, painters and decorators.

On the very day that Mr. Cordyce received word that it was finished, he suggested the drive.

"Do you live all alone, Grandfather?" asked Benny.

"All alone," answered Mr. Cordyce. "No company at all." At first Benny did not consider this the exact truth. He considered a cook company, and also a butler, and a housekeeper. And when he saw the array of maids he kept perfectly quiet. The house was enormous, certainly. It was at least a quarter of a mile from its own front gate—and everywhere were gardens.

"Do you live here?" said Henry, thunderstruck, as they rolled quietly along the beautiful drive.

"You do, too, if you like it," observed his grandfather, watching his face.

The inside of the house was more wonderful than even the older children had ever dreamed. The velvet rugs were so thick and soft that no footfall could be heard. Everywhere were flowers. The great stairway with steps of marble rose from the center of the big hallway. But it was upstairs that the children felt most at home.

Here the rooms were not quite so large. They were sunny and homelike.

"This is Violet's room!" cried Benny. It was unmistakable. There were violets on the wallpaper. The bed was snow white with a thick quilt of violet silk. On the little table were English violets, pouring their fragrance into the room.

"What a beautiful room!" sighed Violet, sinking down into one of the soft cushioned chairs.

But all the children shouted when they saw Benny's room. The wallpaper was blue, covered with large figures of cats and dogs, the Three Bears, and Peter Rabbit. There was a swinging rocking-horse, nearly as large as a real horse, a blackboard, a tool chest, and low tables and chairs exactly the right size for Benny. There was an electric train with cars nearly as large as the little boy himself.

"Can I run the cars all day?" asked Benny.

"Oh, no," replied Henry quickly. "You're going to school as soon as it begins."

This was the first that his grandfather had heard about school, but he agreed with Henry, and chuckled to himself.

"The finest schools in the country," he said. This came true, for all the children finally went to the public schools, and are they not the finest schools in the country?

In Jess' room Benny discovered a bed for Watch. It was, in fact, a regular dog's straw hamper, but it was lined with heavy quilted silk and padded with wool. Watch got in at once, sniffed in every corner, turned around three times, and lay down.

Just then a distant doorbell rang. It had such a low, musical chime that the children listened delightedly, never once giving a thought as to who it might be.

But almost at once a soft-footed servant appeared, saying that a man wanted to see Mr. Cordyce "about the dog." The moment Jess heard that word "dog" she was frightened. She had never thought Watch a common runaway dog, and it always made her uncomfortable to see passers-by gaze curiously at him as he ran by her side.

"They won't take the Watch away?" she whispered to Henry, her breath almost gone.

"Indeed they will not!" declared Henry. "We'll never, never give him up."

However, Henry followed his grandfather and Jess with great anxiety.

It was indeed about Watch that the man wanted to talk, and Jess' heart sank again when she saw the dog jump delightedly upon the man, and return his caresses with short barks.

"He's a runaway, sir, from my kennels out in Townsend," the man explained to Mr. Cordyce. "I have two hundred Airedales out there, and this one was sold the day before he ran away. So you see I have to turn him over to the lady I sold him to."

"Oh, no, you don't," returned Mr. Cordyce quickly. "I will give you three times what the dog is worth."

The man glanced around uneasily. "I couldn't do that, sir," he explained. "You see, it isn't a question of money; it's a question of my promised word to the lady."

Mr. Cordyce failed to "see." "She can find another dog, among two hundred Airedales, I guess," he returned. "And, besides, you don't know positively that this is the right dog."

"Excuse me," replied the man, very much embarrassed, "he's the dog, all right. He knows me, as you see. His name is Rough No. 3. He has a black spot inside his ear."

It was too true. Indeed, at the mere mention of his name the dog cocked an ear and wagged his tail. But he had seated himself as close to Jess as possible, and licked her hand when she patted him.

But it appeared that Henry could understand the man's position even if Mr. Cordyce could not. He now put in a timid word of his own.

"If the lady would agree to let the dog go, would you be willing?"

"Sure," said the man, shooting a glance at Henry.

"I almost know any one would let us keep Watch, Grandfather," said Henry earnestly, "if they knew how much he had done for us."

"I'm sure of it, my boy," returned Mr. Cordyce kindly.

The fact that Henry had been the first to make headway with the dog fancier, had not escaped him.

But it was clear that Jess would not be able to sleep until the matter had been settled, so the moment the man had gone, the children set out from their beautiful new home to the address of the lady who had bought Watch.

The big car purred along from Greenfield to Townsend in no time. And the whole family, including Watch himself, trooped up the veranda steps to interview the lady who held it in her power to break their hearts, or to make them very happy.

She was not terrible to look at. In fact she was quite young, quite lively, and very, very pretty. She asked them all to sit down, which they did gravely, for even Benny was worried about losing "Watchie," his favorite pillow. He could not wait for his grandfather to begin. He struggled down from his chair and dashed over to the young lady saying, in one breath, "You'll let us keep Watchie, please, won't you, because we want him so bad, and Jess didn't know he was your dog?"

By degrees the lady understood just what dog it was.

"We have had him so long," explained Henry, eagerly, "it would be almost like letting Benny go away. Watch never leaves us even for a minute, ever since Jess took the briar out of his foot."

"So you are the children who lived in the freight car!" observed the lively young lady. "I've heard all about that. How did you like it?"

"All right," replied Henry, with an effort. "But we never could have done it without Watch. He stayed and looked after the girls while I was away, and he just thinks everything of Jess."

"Well," said the young lady, laughing, "I can see you're worrying terribly about that dog. Now listen! I wouldn't take that dog away from you any more than I'd take Benny! In fact, not so much. I think maybe I'd like to keep Benny instead."

Benny was apparently quite willing that she should. He climbed into her lap before any one could stop him, and gave her one of his best bear hugs. And from that moment they were firm friends. But the children always spoke of her as the "lady who owns Watch," although Mr. Cordyce paid for the dog in less time than you can imagine. It made no difference to the children that Watch was a very valuable dog. They had loved him when he had not been worth a cent; and now they loved him more, simply because they had so nearly lost him.

It was a happy and reunited family which gathered around the Cordyce dining table that evening. The maids smiled in the kitchen to hear the children laugh; and the children laughed because Watch actually sat up at the table in the seat of honor beside Jess, and was waited upon by a butler.

SAFE

Would you ever dream that four children could be homesick in such a beautiful house as Mr. Cordyce's? Jess was the first one to long for the old freight car.

"O Grandfather," she said one morning, "I wish I could cook something once more in the old kettle."

"Go out in the kitchen," said her grandfather, "and mess around all you like. The maids will help you."

Jess brightened up at once, and flew out into the kitchen, where three or four maids brought her everything she wanted to cook with.

And Benny was the last one to wish for his old home.

"Grandfather," he said one day, "I wish I could drink this milk out of my own pink cup!"

This set Mr. Cordyce to thinking. He had plenty of pink cups, it is true, but none of them were as dear to Benny as his own.

"I think I shall have to surprise your children," said Mr. Cordyce at last. "But before the surprise comes, perhaps you would like to see Benny's pony." Then he led the way to the stables. He owned several beautiful horses already, and nearly a dozen wonderful cars. But nothing was half so interesting as the pony. He was very small and very fat and black. His wavy tail was so long that it nearly touched the ground. And his name was "Cracker," because his birthday fell on the Fourth of July, when firecrackers were popping.

Benny took a short ride around the stable, being "held on" by a groom. But the second time around, he said, "Cracker doesn't need you to hold onto him, I shouldn't wonder," and trotted around with great delight, without help.

All the others sat down on the fragrant hay to watch him ride.

"What am I going to do when I grow up, Grandfather?" asked Henry.

"You're going to take my place, Henry, as president of the steel mills," replied Mr. Cordyce. "You will do it better than I ever have." (And one day this came true, just as most of Mr. Cordyce's prophecies did.)

"And what am I going to do?" asked Jess, curiously.

"All you children must go to school and then to college. Then you may do whatever you choose for a living," replied Mr. Cordyce. (This also came true.)

"Of course I have more than enough money to support us all," went on Mr. Cordyce, "but if you have something to do, you will be happier." (This not only came true, but it is always and forever true, all over the world.)

"Am I going to college tomorrow?" asked Benny, stopping his little pony in front of the group.

"Not tomorrow, Benny," said his grandfather, laughing. "But I'm glad you reminded me. All you children must go over to Dr. McAllister's tomorrow, and stay while the surprise comes."

"Is the surprise very nice?" asked Benny.

"No, not very," replied Mr. Cordyce with a twinkle.

"Did it cost a great deal?" asked Jess.

"It didn't cost me anything," answered her grandfather. "The only thing I shall have to pay will be express." (He didn't tell them that the express cost him several hundred dollars.)

However, the next day the children rode gladly over to see the kind doctor. They stayed until Mr. Cordyce telephoned to them that the surprise was ready. And then Mrs. McAllister and her son rode back with them in the big car.

Mr. Cordyce was as happy as a boy. He led the merry little procession out through his many gardens, past the rose garden, through the banks of purple asters. Then they came to an Italian garden with a fountain in the middle, and a shady little wood around the edge. Among the trees was the surprise. It was an old freight car! The children rushed over to it with cries of delight, pushed back the dear old door, and scrambled in. Everything was in place. Here was Benny's pink cup, and here was his bed. Here was the old knife which had cut butter and bread, and vegetables, and firewood, and string, and here were the letters for Benny's primer. Here was the big kettle and the tablecloth. And hanging on a near-by tree was the old dinner bell. Benny rang the bell over and over again, and Watch rolled on the floor and barked himself hoarse.

The children were never homesick after that. To be sure, a dull and ugly freight car looked a little strange in a beautiful Italian garden. But it was never dull or ugly to the Cordyce children or their dog. They never were so happy as when showing visitors each beauty of their beloved old home. And there were many visitors. Some of them were fascinated by the stories of the wonderful dishes and the shelf. And the children never grew tired of telling them over and over again.

One summer day, many years afterward, Watch climbed out of his beautiful padded silk bed, and barked until Henry lifted him into the freight car. There he lay down on the hard, splintery floor, blinking his eyes in the sun, and watching the children as they sat studying by the fountain.

"He likes the old home best," said Jess Cordyce, smiling at him and patting his rough back.

And as Benny would say, if he hadn't grown up, "That's true, I shouldn't wonder."

ABOUT THE BOOK

The Boxcar Children is a children's book series originally created and written by the American first-grade school teacher Gertrude Chandler Warner.

Warner once said that she did much of her writing while convalescing from illnesses or accidents, and that she conceived the idea of The Boxcar Children while sick at home. Of this, she said –

"I had to stay at home from school because of an attack of bronchitis. Having written a series of eight books to order for a religious organization, I decided to write a book just to suit myself. What would I like to do? Well, I would like to live in a freight car, or a caboose. I would hang my wash out on the little back piazza and cook my stew on the little rusty stove found in the caboose."

On July 3, 2004, the Gertrude Chandler Warner Boxcar Children Museum opened in Putnam, Connecticut. It is located across the street from Warner's childhood home and is housed in an authentic 1920s New Haven R.R. boxcar. The museum is dedicated to Warner's life and work, and includes original signed books, photos and artifacts from her life and career as a teacher in Putman. Included is the desk at which a 9-year-old Warner wrote her first story titled Golliwog at the Zoo. There is also a re-creation of the living space created by the Aldens – the Boxcar Children themselves.

ABOUT THE AUTHOR

Gertrude Chandler Warner (April 16, 1890 – August 30, 1979) was an American author, mainly of children's stories. She was most famous for writing the original book of **The Boxcar Children** and for the next eighteen books in the series.

From the age of five, Warner dreamed of being an author, and began writing in ten-cent blank books as soon as she was able to hold a pencil. Her first book was an imitation of Florence Kate Upton's Golliwog stories and was titled Golliwog at the Zoo. It "consisted of verses illustrated with watercolors of the two Dutch clocks and the Golliwag." Warner presented this book to her grandfather, and every Christmas afterwards, she would give him a hand-made book as a present.

Warner was a lover of nature. While growing up, she had butterfly and moth collections, pressed wildflowers, learned of all the birds in her area, and kept a garden. She used these interests in teaching her grade school students, and also used nature themes in her books. For instance, in the second book of The Boxcar Children (Surprise Island), the Alden children make a nature museum from the flowers, shells and seaweed they have collected and the shapes of birds they have observed. One of her students recalled the wildflower and stone-gathering contests that Warner sponsored when she was a teacher.

Made in the USA
Middletown, DE
03 April 2023

28164984R00060